MW00846866

Praise for

Dulcified, Sweetened by the Education of Life
by Lisa R. Ramirez, Ed.D

"*Dulcified* should be required reading for all educators. Dr. Ramirez' story powerfully depicts how relationships can significantly impact the life path of individuals. The kindness, caring, and unconditional acceptance of one teacher becomes one of the life altering experiences that strengthens the spirit within and carries Dr. Ramirez to the height of success that is now her reality. *Dulcified* carries a compelling message for all educators."

> – GEORGIA GRIJALVA, faculty
> advisor, CalStateTEACH, San Jose
> State University Educational
> Administration Master's Program

"*Dulcified* is an absolutely riveting book! It will take you on a tour of the life of a courageous and resolute young girl who despite the deplorable acts forced upon her, not only survived but thrived! This is absolutely a must read for any person suffering abuse and/or neglect and feels trapped. While the story is heart-breaking; the whole picture will leave you searching for someone to help, a reason to reach out, and a chance to be Dulcified by life!"

> – LENA CLOE, victim assistance
> coordinator/advocate, Lynn County
> (Tahoka, TX)

"The words, 'To walk in Victory' describe Dr. Lisa Ramirez. Her book takes the reader to both the spiritual and practical side of leadership and to a place far beyond the heart...the soul. This is a must read for both new and experienced teachers in understanding the diverse situations their students face on a daily basis, or anyone looking for a ray of hope to face another day. I plan on incorporating this book into my diversity curriculum for pre-service teachers. May they begin to understand the world that so many of our precious children live in, and be able to make a difference... like Dr. Ramirez."

> – ANNETTE E. SMITH, M. Ed.,
> coordinator, Associates of Arts in
> Teaching Program, South Plains
> College

"Dulcified is a powerful story of one woman's spiritual journey with God. Lisa talks about her very abusive and neglected childhood in an uncensored and raw way it makes your teeth clinch. However, her love for God and her determination to rise above through education are so powerful they shine through on every page. A must read for not only educators, but anyone who works with children, and can positively impact that child's life."

> – MEGAN SOLIZ, research assistant

"Joy, sadness, love and forgiveness come together flawlessly in this book. *Dulcified* deals with intense issues such as physical abuse, poverty and sexual abuse. Issues, many children in our schools face today. *Dulcified* is an exceptional and extraordinary account of sheer will and determination to survive. Dr. Ramirez shares with her readers how to take life by the horns and be all that God intends us to be. Thank you, Dr. Lisa Ramirez for your bravery and stepping out to help others overcome the odds."

– MARY ANN JUAREZ, grant
programs coordinator, Snyder ISD

"I have been an educator for over 18 years and have read countless books throughout my personal and professional career; however, very few books have left such an impression on me as *Dulcified*. Dr. Ramirez' life story will make you laugh and cry but most notably it will persuade you to be a better person. *Dulcified* demonstrates that anyone can overcome even the most difficult circumstances and triumph. I have always tried to 'pay it forward', but *Dulcified* reinvigorated my passion for making a difference in the lives of my students!"

– EDNA R. GARCIA, federal programs
administrator

"A triumph of the human spirit! The author overcomes unspeakable childhood abuse and impoverished living conditions to end up with a dulcified life. Through her inspiring journey of spirituality, compassion, and forgiveness, she teaches the reader how an education can save lives."

> — RENA YASSIRI, training and process improvement manager, Navy Marine-Corps Relief Society

"Dr. Ramirez gives us a tool to reach students that are in need and crying inside. *Dulcified* moved me spiritually to another level. She was able to give life a deeper, divine purpose. It is a must read. This book gives hope to our youth and individuals facing daily challenges."

> — DARYL L. MACKEY, educator and author of *Teamesteem™ is the Key to a Teen's Financial Dreams*

"My colleagues and I all read this book in one evening, then passed on our copies to others. We did so not by coordinated effort, but because that is what the book compelled us to do. It must be read and it must be shared with all who might perpetuate its clear messages about the kinds of help that are most effective.

Dulcified is not only motivating, it is capable of guiding culture and policy within groups of people. I lived most of my life wondering where the people were who survived the things that I did, and was told by professionals that they didn't exist. I was told that they either killed themselves or did the risky or purposeful things they needed to do to be killed by others. They do exist, and hopefully this book will start the conversation about how we can help others to create the conditions where surviving can turn to thriving."

> – SUSAN STENTZ, M.Ed., behavior support specialist/former teacher and school administrator, Fairfax County Public Schools, former instructor and university supervisor, George Mason University

"I couldn't put the book down once I started reading it, and I couldn't quit thinking about it after I finished. A powerful story of hope that gives insight into the world many of our students live in and reveals the negative and positive impact adults can have on a child. I definitely recommend it."

> – DR. RANDY BROWN, superintendent, Snyder ISD

Dulcified

Sweetened by the Education of Life

Lisa R. Ramírez, Ed.D.

TP REWARDS

Dulcified
Copyright © 2011 by Lisa R. Ramírez.
All rights reserved.

Published by TP Rewards LLC
8647 Richmond Highway #659
Alexandria, VA 22309
www.tp-rewards.com

No part of this publication may be reproduced, stored in a
retrieval system or transmitted in any way by any means,
electronic, mechanical, photocopy, recording or otherwise
without written permission of the publisher except as provided
by USA copyright law.

Scripture quotations are taken from the *Holy Bible, New Living
Translation*, copyright © 1996, 2004, 2007. Used by permission
of Tyndale House Publishers, Inc., Carol Stream, Illinois 60188.
All rights reserved.

Book design by TP Rewards LLC
Cover photo by Kaitlyn Ramírez.
Author photo by Mike Ramírez.

International Standard Book Number: 978-0-9838242-5-1
Library of Congress Control Number: 2011936890

Published in the United States of America

This book is dedicated to my daughter, Kaitlyn, because Judy Blume p***** her off.

***

I would like to acknowledge that Kaitlyn is the photographer responsible for the image on the cover of this book. My Baby Girl is "ah-mazing"—I love you! This book is also dedicated to Drina because without her demonstrated courage, I would not have been brave enough to move forward with this project. To my precious mother for giving me her blessing and permission to share this story. To my siblings, for together, we represent what God can accomplish. To my spiritual mentors, especially Mr. James V. Baker, I send my eternal gratitude. To my unconditional friends, including my Kappa Delta Chi sisters, who have inspired me and placed their trust and confidence in my abilities, mil gracias. To my son, whose sheer existence and curiosity demonstrates God's goodness and possibility. And especially to my strong, unassuming, and so very funny husband, Mike—without his brutal honesty and ability to hold me accountable, I would never have started this book, much less seen it to fruition. And of course, to my Heavenly Father, as found in Psalms 9:1-2:

"I will praise you, Lord, with all my heart; I will tell of all the marvelous things you have done.

I will be filled with joy because of you. I will sing praises to your name, O Most High."

Contents

part two

part three

Foreword

Lisa has always been special. From the beginnings of our friendship, it was evident that she had a gift for meeting people where they were at, accepting them for who they were and not fearing who or what they had been. It was obvious to me that God used Lisa to love people who some might call unlovable; to make a difference in those lives she touched. <u>Dulcified</u> is the story of Lisa's ongoing journey to overcome seemingly impossible odds, becoming the resilient, remarkable woman she is today.

I met Lisa during a time of firsts for both of

us. We had the opportunity to work in a small rural economically disadvantaged school on the South Plains of Texas, I as a first time counselor and she as a new teacher to the district. Lisa was coming home; this was the school that she attended many times throughout those difficult years of her childhood. This was the same high school that she was once expelled from. The superintendent who hired her to teach 10th and 11th grade English was the same caring and compassionate man who had been forced to expel her. I am very sure he felt that was one of the best hiring decisions he ever made. She was and still is one of the best teachers I have ever had the opportunity to observe. Her students adored her, but more importantly they learned from her. She made them believe that through education the possibilities for them were endless.

As an assistant principal in our elementary school and later a principal in a larger district, she brought a sense of excitement and passion to all around her. She was able to motivate and encourage teachers and students, a living example of how God can use us in our brokenness to inspire. This remarkable young woman, who had every reason to give up, was the catalyst to create positive change in the environment around her. When she felt led to apply for a job in Washington D.C. with the United States Department of Education, she hesitated, wondering how she could make a difference there. She has, as the Director of Migrant Education, brought a true reality of who these children are and how the policies created by our government impacts them and their communities. She has inspired and required those with whom she works to "see" the children not just as numbers on a page but as the future of this richly diverse country. To recognize that no matter what that child's beginnings or life experiences, each has the potential for greatness if given opportunity.

Lisa almost did not pursue the job in Washington. She had gone through all of the red tape to apply, but had not heard anything. It was just prior to leaving to attend my last high school banquet and prom as an administrator that I received her call. I remember sitting on my bathroom floor listening to her concern that, since she had not heard anything from the USDE, the job must not have been in God's plan for her and her family. I remember wondering what I could say to support this friend I loved so much. Then through no plan or thought of my own, the words came. I encouraged her to call the current Director of Migrant Education. "You have his number, or it must be on the website. What could it hurt to call?" She eventually did make that call, actually talked to the Director himself and found that she was still being considered. God needed Lisa in Washington and used a simple phone call to get that done.

Lisa brings a richness and compassion to

the lives of those around her, and we are better because of that gift. When I was diagnosed with cancer, Lisa cried and laughed with me. In my vanity, losing my hair was traumatic. So when Lisa showed up at my door as bald as I was, I was indescribably humbled. I realized then that God uses people to demonstrate His love for us, even in the darkest times. We just have to allow Him to use us for that higher purpose. Lisa allows God to use her in dramatic ways to inspire, and give hope to all of us.

May you come to know Dr. Lisa Ramírez and her love for God through reading <u>Dulcified</u>, and may the experience enrich and bless your life, as knowing and loving Lisa has mine.

Sherri Brooks McCord, M.Ed.
Education Specialist/Accountability Solutions

Preface

*11 For he will command his angels concerning you
to guard you in all your ways;
12 they will lift you up in their hands,
so that you will not strike your foot against a stone.*

Psalm 91:11-12

Dulcified recounts the battles that have
been won and lost as I have sailed before the wind
through the chronicle of this brief life. It goes back
to my earliest memories and puts into focus the
kaleidoscope of colors that have served to either

brighten or singe my soul's embroidered edges. The story I share is not always pleasant but it is indeed beautiful. As you read through this book, please know that the end product is simply a brief recollection of a few memories. The major events that I recount did happen and the characters in the story did actually exist, though many of them under different names. However, since so many years have come to pass, the actual conversations could not be repeated verbatim nor the details fully visualized, but I have tried to capture them the way I experienced them. It is not my desire or intention to hurt anyone or place judgment on any individual.

I must also add a little disclaimer before you read any further. This book does contain some strong language and sensitive content. Note that my rationale for sharing in such detail is simply to allow you as the reader to have insight to the severity of many of the situations that played out in my earliest days. I have attempted to "tone it down" a bit as the true purpose of this book is to share a story that bears witness to God's mercy and goodness. The many angels that He has set in my path over the years have blessed me beyond articulation. At the end of the day, I am a regular, everyday person that struggles like everyone else so you should know that I am humbled by this endeavor. It is my sincere desire that this beam of light reach the readers in the manner it was intended, and may they feel His warmth and His mighty hand of protection as they move forward in faith.

Introduction

First of all, I never wanted to write this book. The reason I am writing this book is because I am responding to the requests that I have received over the years from audience members that have attended my talks and seminars. Part I will take you through a series of memories, both joyful and painful, that cumulatively tell a story of lived life experiences that have ultimately resulted in an abundantly blessed life and career. As raw as the content is and as very vulnerable and exposed I feel every time I share this story, there has *always* been at least one individual who has come up to me afterward to tell me that they too had similar experiences and that they had been silently living in shame for the majority of their lives. These individuals have been male and female, young and old, married and single, educated and non-educated, parents, teachers and students, from every race and ethnicity—the thing they have in common is that they hurt and they seek freedom from their past. This book is intended specifically for educators, and educational leaders but it is equally relevant for individuals that seek to understand how every child, regardless of their physical, cultural, and environmental circumstances, deserves to be seen through the lens of possibility and hope. As educators, we must understand how our own personal experiences often provoke (or tempt) us to see others as inferior when we should be constantly challenging ourselves to stay true to our mission and purpose of social justice through educational attainment. Subsequently, Part II of the book reflects some of the lessons and truths that I have extrapolated both from experiences as an educator and educational leader and through my research in the area of spiritual leadership as it relates to educational leadership. Please note that the information provided regarding my research is summarized; therefore, further discourse on the topic is being captured in another one of my works.

Part III, although brief, serves to tie up

some loose ends for the reader. It allows the reader to know how resolution has been achieved and how absolutely *dulce* (sweet) life truly is. It also illustrates the true gift God gives through the people He places in our lives. Every life has purpose and meaning, the challenge lies in discerning what yours is and helping others accomplish theirs by Paying it Forward.

part one

NOT-So-Sweet Beginnings

In the spring of 2000, I was invited to speak to a group of high school students in Lamesa, Texas as part of their AIM High program. I had no idea what I would say to such a fascinating group of young people. It had been many years since I had been in Lamesa, Texas so in an attempt to help them relate to the story at hand, I began at the only place I knew to start—the beginning.

I am the oldest of five children. We are four girls and one boy; we have four different fathers. My father is a Mexican national and my mother is Mexican American. Although I was born in

Chicago, I only lived there for a short while. I was raised primarily by a single mother and we moved a lot as we worked as migratory agricultural workers and needed to move in search of work several times a year. My mother, who was born in Minnesota, became pregnant with me at the age of eighteen as a result of an affair with a married man. My grandparents, being of the Catholic belief, were very ashamed of her and, basically, disowned her once they learned of her pregnancy. She was faced with a difficult choice to make knowing that if she kept me she risked no longer be considered part of the family. One month after her 19th birthday, she gave birth to me and with love in her heart, she chose to keep me.

In a perfect world, she would have learned her lesson and lived her life in a way that would have been somewhat less controversial, especially since this was during the mid-seventies. But no, undaunted, she gave birth to my sister Sofie three months after my first birthday. Sofie and I did not share the same dad, but we shared everything else. My sister Sofie and I were very close growing up out of mutual admiration and the sheer fact that we needed each other to survive.

My mother, although very capable, did not complete her high school education. She dropped out somewhere around her junior year. The migratory lifestyle of my grandparents had her moving frequently and, eventually, she succumbed to my grandfather's demands for her to quit school in order to work full time and be a contributing member of the family. However, when my grandfather disowned her, she was not allowed to work with the family so she sought work wherever she could find it. I don't know all the different kinds of jobs she took to put food on the table, but I know that being a bartender was one of them. During those days, our family's main source of transportation was a little red Radio Flyer wagon. Occasionally, my mother would stop by a yard sale and allow my sister and me to each pick one item to buy. She would say that she didn't care what we chose as long as it was a book.

It is my mother to whom I attribute my great love for reading. My mother loved to read and would often take the time to tell us about what she was reading whether it was the Bible, a novel or some random trashy magazine. You would be amazed how attentive Sofie and I were during those times, especially when it came to the latest revelations exposed in her *True Confessions* magazines. She would also read little graphic novels in Spanish and she would show us the pictures as she explained all the different scenes to us. We learned to speak English and Spanish at the same time, so I can't really say which language took precedent. She enjoyed explaining to us the process of looking through the classifieds of the newspaper

Dulcified 5

so we could learn to locate the best garage sales in town. My mother was a fun mother in many respects. She was very creative and she knew how to make our dismal surroundings beautiful. She possessed an amazing knack for teaching us how to enjoy opportunities for fun that cost very little to no money.

When it was time for my mother to go to work, she would load Sofie and me into the red Radio Flyer wagon, along with some books and a little blankie, and we would spend occasional evenings underneath the counter in the bar at which she worked.

The hours under the counter were spent reading to Sofie, even though I must admit that I use the term reading loosely. I didn't know how to read but I would tell her what ever story I wanted, just as my mother did for us. I would go through each picture and spin a tale. When that story got old, I would flip the book over and start again from the other end. Sofie was never the wiser, either that or she was just being a really good sport so we could be the "big girls" we were expected to be.

Babysitters

Our young mother hated to have to take us to the bar and, actually, tried to get us a babysitter; but, unfortunately they were either too expensive or too unreliable. Many times she was forced to leave us with whoever said they would watch after us. One particular babysitter, that we shall call Shirley, was just a few years older than I was, yet she was tasked to watch us at our apartment when she got out of school. In the beginning, I liked Shirley. She had long carrot-red hair that she wore loose with a lovely barrette that held half her hair out of her face. She had beautiful dresses and a white parasol with little flowers that she would use to protect her, fair, freckled face. She had big blue eyes that seemed to shine when she was happy. Shirley lived with her grandmother and the two of them only spoke Spanish. I finally had to ask that we not be left with her anymore. You see, Shirley had two very annoying and awkward-to-handle habits.

Her first annoying habit was that she liked to scratch her bottom and then smell it. As if her habit was not disgusting enough, she would try to force us to also smell her finger. She would chase us down and place her finger under our noses. YUCK!

The second annoying habit of hers was that she liked to masturbate, all the time. She would usually use a blanket but sometimes she would use our stuffed animals to make her humping material! Double YUCK!

Of course, I only told my mother about her first annoying habit.

In case you're wondering why I would direct attention to a random bottom-scratching-then-sniffing, masturbating babysitter, I should confide that even she became preferable to what lay ahead for me. If I had known how the scenes in the movie of my life would unfold, I certainly would have chosen Shirley.

Shortly after deciding that Shirley would no longer babysit us, we were left in the care of my mother's Uncle Armando. Not really being of an age at which I could discern the age of others, I would have to say that Armando had to have been in his mid-to-late twenties. Armando spoke to my mother only with kind words and, "Of course, I'd be happy to watch the girls for you, Mija. No, no they will be no problem at all. In fact, since you will be working so late, why don't you come get them tomorrow morning when you wake up since you will be so tired. *No te preocupes*, I'll feed them breakfast."

And so it was. My mother dropped us off at his house on her way to work. I can't recall what we did in the evenings but I certainly remember how our mornings went.

One morning I was awakened by noise in the kitchen so I crawled out of the bed that Sofie and I shared at Armando's house. I walked down the hall toward the kitchen and I rubbed my eyes as I saw him standing in the hallway. He said something to the effect of, "Good morning, are you hungry?" I said, "Yes, can I have some Sugar Pops?" He said, "Sure you can. But first you have to do a little something for me." With that he unzipped his pants and reached into his Fruit of the Looms. He grabbed me by the head and shoved his privates into my mouth and pulled my hair back and forth until he was in a rhythm he found enjoyable. Once he reached the point of satisfaction, he pushed me away, zipped his pants and filled a bowl with Sugar Pops.

Then he sent me to eat my cereal in front of the television, and I sat there eating each piece of cereal one by one, too afraid to ask for milk.

I don't like Sugar Pops.

Lisa R. Ramírez, Ed.D.

I Don't Know Where the Angels Sleep

"Sleep with the angels," she whispered.

That's what my mother always said when she put us to bed. The idea behind it was that we would have sweet dreams because the angels would be protecting us as we slumbered.

As I lay there, I wondered what she and her friends were doing in the kitchen. I enjoyed listening to Barry White blaring on the radio and wished that I could stay up late like she did every night. My mom had all the fun. Her friends came over frequently, always remembering to bring the Oreo cookies for their late night munchies. There they were laughing, drinking Schlitz beer and rolling cigarettes.

I liked her friends even though they never really talked to me or my sister, Sofie. We were simply Maria's kids. Just as if we were her arms, legs, toes, nostrils—whatever. We just were.

I got out of my bed and felt the roughness of the cheap, shag carpet in my tiny bedroom. But it was hot pink with specks of lighter pink and white. Round, round, and round I went. I don't stop until the room is moving. The walls have to go faster, faster, faster. I see the light of the street lamp coming in through the window. The cars are going way too fast down the streets of our Chicago Heights neighborhood. I finally collapse on the carpet, dizzy from the spinning. I can smell the mustiness of the rug and feel its treads as I dig my tiny, five-year-old fingers into the base. I slowly crawl to the door. I want to see what they are doing out there.

I step into the hall and peek around the corner to watch them playing at the kitchen table that is pushed up against the wall of our cramped basement apartment. The radio is sitting on the sill of a window that is located directly above the table. The window is open to let in the cool evening breeze and I can see the feet of the passersby as they go about their raucous night.

And then without warning, I hear a scream, and I see an arm that has reached through the open window and grabbed the black, square radio—I see the electrical cord drifting away like the tail of the kite I saw at the park.

"Son of a b____!" someone said.

And the music was gone, and the party was over. My heart was racing. That scared me. The thought of my mother finding out that I'm out of my bed scares me more. I run back to my room and jump underneath my blankets. I cover my head and hope that she didn't hear me. I hear my breath, I feel my heart beating, and it's really hot under there. I realize that I have a window in my room and its right over my bed. What if someone sticks their arm through that window and takes me?

Sleep with the angels? I start to cry very quietly. For as long as I can remember and probably forever more, I will be plagued by nightmares because I don't know where the angels sleep.

Move to Texas

And so time passed as it always does. Many random images fill my memory when I look back. Some of those images include watching my mother tattoo the words, "Mi <3 " on her left forearm to symbolize her newfound love for the father of her soon-to-be third child, my sister, Ani.

It wasn't long after that night, that a group of four men had carried her into our apartment. Each held a limb with total disregard to the fact that her skirt had ridden up her thighs to expose her underwear. By this point in time, Sofie and I were staying at home alone in the evenings with the instructions to never open the door for anyone—not even her, since she had her own key. Perhaps this explains why I wasn't really frightened when they brought her home. I did, however, become alarmed as I noticed that my beautiful mother had blood on her lip and purple bruising on her face. Her eyes were barely open but she looked right at me and she whispered for me to go to bed. "Go to bed, baby, and lock the door. Take care of your sister."

I hid under my blankets, trembling with fear, as I very attentively listened to the voices of the men I didn't recognize, but was comforted when I heard the voice of my mother's best friend, Alma. Alma was several years older than my mother and had several older children. She was a large, kind woman. Her smiles were so big that they caused her eyes to close. She loved my mother very much and not only because her brother was Sofie's father. She loved all three of us and, in fact, became Sofie's Godmother. That night she became even more special to me as I overheard her telling the men what to do as they cleaned my mother up and placed her safely into her bed.

The next morning, Alma fixed Sofie and me some breakfast and started to counsel my mother. "Chiquilla, you have to do something with your life. You can't keep living like this. You are going to get killed and then what is going to happen to these girls." My mother sobbed as she nodded her head in agreement.

I'm not sure if it was the beating she had received or the news that she was once again pregnant that caused her to try to settle down. She quit her job at the bar and cleaned houses instead. I assume that she was also on public assistance because I don't know how else she would have been able to keep food on the table.

Occasionally, my father would visit bearing gifts for both Sofie and me. He was still married to his wife and had no intention of ever leaving her but he wanted to see me and "help however he could." His visits were always brief but pleasant. He would sweep me up into his arms and turn on the record player full blast and dance. My favorite record was *Before the Next Teardrop Falls* by Freddy Fender.

My mother appeared happier and more beautiful as she started to show from her third pregnancy. One afternoon she got all of us dressed up and took Sofie and me to the local drugstore to have our photo taken. It seemed like happy times.

Shortly after we took that photo, my mother received a phone call from my grandfather informing my mother that my great-grandfather had passed away. I'm not a hundred percent sure how the story goes but this is how it has been retold to me. He asked my mother to come to Texas to attend the funeral, but because of the expense we could not go with her. She was hopeful that somehow the trip would allow her to become part of my grandfather's family again.

While she was there, she met a man that extended to her the opportunity to, once again, become a "good woman" and be part of the family. She was to marry the man; he happened to live in a farmhouse near my grandfather's house where he was working as a farmhand. He had recently divorced and was responsible for four sons. The man was significantly older than my twenty-four-year-old mother, but in her sorrow and earnest desire to be accepted back into my grandfather's good graces, she accepted.

Upon my mother's return to Chicago Heights, she informed us that we were going to have a father and brothers and a house to live in and that we would get to meet our grandparents and life was going to be good for us. And so it was, when I was five we got rid of what little possessions we owned and carried only what could be taken on the Greyhound bus and headed to Lubbock, Texas. Alma's daughter, Mita, knitted Sofie and me little red and white purses that we could use for our trip to Texas. At the bus station, my mother hugged her precious friend, Alma, as if she would never see her again. Alma said goodbye by giving my mother a *bendición* and tracing the sign of the cross on all of our foreheads.

As the Greyhound bus took us down the endless highway more miles away from Chicago

Heights than we had ever been, Sofie and I took small, little bites of the tacos Alma had packed for us because we weren't sure where we were going or when we would eat again. We quietly read to each other and played patty-cake. Sofie and I held hands as we slept until my mother gently woke us up to let us know that we had arrived.

My poor, sweet mother. She had such high hopes. How was she to know that moving to Texas would open up the doors to a living hell?

Family Matters

After we left the bus station in Lubbock, Texas we drove to a farm located near the little town of O'Donnell, Texas. O'Donnell's claim to fame is being the hometown of Dan Blocker, better known as Hoss Cartwright from the television series *Bonanza*.

It was late night and only two of my soon-to-be stepbrothers were there, James, the oldest, and Anthony who was just two years older than I was, so he was seven. Anthony sat with me on the recliner and tried to be nice and share his toy gun with me but I wasn't having it. I was very tired, hungry and uncomfortable in my new surroundings. Sofie and I refused to take off our coats and shoes. We even kept our hats on as we watched my mother dance with the man that would become her husband.

I heard Jose Alfredo Jimenez's "Te Solté La Rienda" but it was Yolanda Del Rio's "La Hija De Nadie" that made me sad because I knew even then that I would always be nobody's daughter.

The next day we had a big Tex-Mex cookout, the kind where you kill a goat and nail it to the tree and save the blood in foil so you can eat it when it's crisp. It appeared that people came out of the woodwork. And of course everyone was "related." We heard things like "She's your *tia* from the *tio's* side. This is your *primo/prima*. Be nice to each other, you're related, now go play. And don't be where the men are *porque no se mira bien*," (it doesn't look right). After a few weekends like this, I learned how it worked. Everyone is invited; there are lots of foods and lots of beer. The women cook inside and gossip and the men sit outside and get drunk and talk about manly things. I also learned that when my *Tios* were drunk they offered us money to run and get them another beer. We children ran in and out of doors playing wherever they wanted with the understanding that we were expected to stay out of the way.

"But when does the party end?" you ask. Well, my friends, the party ends when the beer has run out and the first fight begins. This was a new and strange phenomenon for us because my mother had always tried to protect us from being witness to such scenes. Unfortunately, her ability to shelter us did not last long. My mother was 4'11 and 100 pounds soaking wet. Her new husband was around 5'10 and weighed about 220 lbs. She was simply no match for him.

One late Saturday night after everyone had left our house, they stayed up arguing and yelling, which frightened me so I stayed up to make sure she was OK. The next thing I knew, I saw my mother fly across the room one way and then again the other way. He had struck her with such force that he propelled her into the air. She landed in the glass window of the living room and was motionless. Instantly, I saw blood coming out from beneath her head. I rushed over to her and started screaming for her to speak to me. She was unconscious and could not respond. The next thing I remember seeing was a little dark image rushing past me and landing right on his chest: Sofie. She was so angry that she attacked him and was hitting him with all her little might. He responded by swiftly slapping her in the face hard enough to leave a mark and tossing her on the floor next to where I was sitting over my mother.

I stared at Sofie and I could tell that the anger she was carrying was not gone and that she was in pain. But her pride and her stubbornness would not allow her to cry. She and I turned our mother over and started to pick the glass out of her face. She and I worked on her for what seemed like hours; interestingly enough, my stepbrothers never came out of their room. I looked over at her husband to see if he was going to help or say sorry or do something. But no, he just finished his beer, crushed the aluminum can and went to bed.

Sofie and I wiped my mother's face and head with a wet towel until the three of us fell asleep on the hard wood floor with the lights on and the music blaring.

My mother woke up early the next morning and started to sweep the glass, straighten up the living room, clean out ash trays and fix breakfast. By noon, our house was spotless and smelled of Pine-Sol and Clorox. She had put everything "back in order" and resumed life as if nothing had ever happened the night before. She and her husband were as lovey-dovey as ever.

What I didn't know then, but certainly know now, is that her necessity to always have a highly organized, sterile and super functional home was her only way of having any semblance of control in her life. If I had only known, I would have been able to recognize the tell-tale signs of illness then; but, it wasn't until many years after I left home that she was diagnosed and treated for obsessive-compulsive disorder (OCD) and manic depression. Unfortunately, she suffered alone in those days without proper medical care and not even one single friend to help bear witness to her struggle.

As the domestic abuse increased in intensity and frequency, I noticed a marked difference in my mother. My once happy, glowing, beautiful mother began to slowly deteriorate. She was often sad and did not seem to be able to remember simple things like our names, what we were making for dinner, or what book she had promised to read with us. She started eating less and less and at one point was down to 76 pounds. Sometimes she was often the last one to go to sleep and the first to be up making meals or sewing, but then other times she would sleep entire days away. It was very difficult to gauge what her moods would be like from hour-to-hour much less day-to-day.

Other times, she would be hyper-energized and would embark on the deep cleaning of our house even if it was two in the morning. Unfortunately, anytime she was cleaning, it meant that we were helping. She would pull all of the dishes out of the cupboards and demand they all be rewashed and dried. All items in the pantry had to be reorganized and clothes in the closet had to be in just the right order. Walls and floorboards would need to be scrubbed and floors polished. During these times she would have very little control of her temper. Her agitation and frustration with us would quickly explode into fits of rage accompanied by verbal and physical lashings. The words she would say would cut to my very soul, but even then imagining a life without her in it was more than my heart could bear. So, you can imagine the outright despair I experienced when we were separated from her due to her nervous breakdowns and a suicide attempt.

My mother is special to me for a variety of reasons. I love her very much and I have an admiration for her ability to endure all she has endured. I learned some of my strongest family values from my mother. Some of those values include worshipping God, being respectful and kind to all people, humility, and expressing love through generosity with time and money. There were many instances when my mother would drive to the homes of elderly people she had befriended and invite them over for dinner especially during the holidays. Many afternoons she could be found brushing their hair or clipping their nails. She would bring Sofie, Ani and me along and we would help clean up their homes and prepare meals. She would also clean their yard and wash their laundry. Through her actions, she demonstrated being kind and respectful to our elders. Money was never something she had much of, but she was generous with what she had. She often reminded us that, even if we had little of our own, we were very fortunate and that in all things we should give thanks to God and know that it could always be worse.

Scared

Every single kind of abuse that you can imagine happened in that home. I am sickened when I think about how adults in positions of authority over children sometimes choose to use that authority to engage them in the most dastardly and perverse acts. I am even more disturbed when I think about how they are able to do it with such stealth and slyness that the unsuspecting child thinks nothing of it.

In the late 70s, *Jaws* was televised by ABC for the first time. I was so excited that I was allowed to stay up to watch it. My mother's husband said he would stay up with me so I wouldn't be scared. I should have thought something of it, as everyone else was sent to bed early, including my mother.

Somewhere in the middle of the Great White Shark making the beach town of Amity his personal feeding ground and Hooper and Quint going out to kill it, my mother's husband managed to place my hand on his genitals and sneak his massive hand into my panties. Before the night had ended it was necessary for me to run to the bathroom and wash out my mouth.

As I stood in the bathroom, I was mindful to stay away from the toilet in case Jaws came up through the commode and to keep the door locked in case my mother's husband decided to come in through the door. Both of them were equally terrifying.

Such occurrences became more and more frequent. He found pleasure in making me stand by the toilet to watch him masturbate so that I could learn the proper technique. It wasn't long before he made excuses to have me with him as much as possible. He would tell my mother that I needed to go with him on the tractor while he plowed the fields so I could learn how to drive and how to work.

On those particular days, he would take extended breaks and have me sit in the cab of his pickup as he performed various unspeakable acts on my prepubescent body. Then he would finish the days off by forcing me to perform various equally perverse acts on him. The taste of Pepsi heated by 110 degree weather that I used to rinse his fluids out of my mouth would be burning in my mouth by the time we got to the driveway. Before I was ever let out of the pickup I was very menacingly reminded that if I were to tell anyone that he would kill my mother. He would also add that Sofie, Ani, and I would be left alone in the world because nobody wanted us, not even our fathers. After witnessing everything I had seen, I had no reason to believe that he couldn't or wouldn't do it. And that is how my uncanny skill of learning to suffer in silence began. I never fought and I never told a soul until many years later.

Good Times

Believe it or not, not all things were bad even in the midst of all that was happening around us. There were glimpses of good times and sheer joy as we survived our childhood by being children. One particular scene is imprinted in my mind forever, but it actually speaks to my earliest days of wanting to be a witness for God.

"Don't let the *pollitos* (baby chicks) out while we're gone," she said as she was getting into the yellow Toyota to make a trip to the grocery store in the metropolis of O'Donnell, Texas (population 1,200 in the mid-seventies).

Two of my stepbrothers, my sister Sofie and I were all swimming in the steel stock tank that we used to hold water for the cattle. The heat had to have been in the low hundreds in mid-spring. I remember it being Easter time because we had recently watched *Jesus of Nazareth* on television. I remember being so fascinated by the concept of being washed of your sins by water baptism. I had even practiced in the tub at night: "In the name of the Father, and of the Son, and of the Holy Spirit…"

James and Anthony splashed Sofie and me in a pool that was much too shallow but it was still better than swimming in the ditch. Just as soon as we noticed that the Toyota was gone over the hill, we all jumped out of the tank to let the *pollitos* out. There were several yellow baby chicks and one little black chick. They scurried around as we chased them around the farm yard. We were barefoot and we had to be careful because the stickers were abundant. We were dripping the algae-laden water and the big drops seemed to frighten the chicks even more. We decided to play a game in which the person who first captured the black chick would be the winner. So we laughed and giggled and pushed and shoved as soon as one of us got close to the black chick. Sofie, the most athletically inclined, was sure to win. Several times she was right on the verge of catching the little critter and we would yell and scream in hopes of frightening the chick so it would scramble away. And then she reached out her swift, pinto-brown hands to catch the chick and "someone" (not me!) pushed her from behind. She attempted to catch her balance but it was too late—her plump, bare foot landed right on top of the little black chick and squish, it was dead.

"Ew." Followed by, "You're gonna get in trouble!" We were eerily quiet as the three of us looked up at her and down at the dead chick. Anthony in all his wisdom informed her that she was going to hell. Sofie started to cry, partly because she was sad about the chick, partly because she was going to hell, but mainly because she wanted to get the chick guts off her foot.

To help her with her dilemma, we advised her to get back in the stock tank to wash off her foot. We joined her and, as solemnly as any church service I've ever attended, I announced that indeed there was a way to save her. She would need to be baptized. James, Anthony and I discussed it at length in quiet whispers with intentional loud words, such as "Eternal Damnation" and "Chick Killer."

We finally returned to her and asked her if she was sorry for her sins. When she affirmed that she was repentant, we instructed her to cross her arms across her chest as we took turns pinching her nose and submerging her into the water, "In the Name of the Father, and of the Son, and of the Holy Spirit." And just for good measure, we continued to baptize her until she nearly drowned.

That evening as we sat around the dinner table, we stole little glances at each other as we smiled with great pride at a very tired and red-eyed Sofie because yes, a chick had died, but at least Sofie's soul had been saved.

***

Living in West Texas has one noticeable drawback—sandstorms! The winds can pick up to amazing speeds, and because the land is primarily made up of wide-open spaces the dirt has no choice but to be tossed around mercilessly. Even some of the best sealed windows and doors will be left with mounds of sand after such an event. Cotton can be torn to shreds and the paint and windshields on vehicles get literally sandblasted. If you mix in the temperature on top of sand, you get one hot mess.

More often than not, the migrant housing we lived in was not properly insulated so the sand flew indoors almost as freely as it did outdoors. True to my mother's optimistic nature, she never complained, she just figured out ways to make the best of it.

"Kids, get your shoes on. We're going outside."

All of us looked at her in amazement. The wind had to be blowing at least forty miles an hour and visibility was extremely limited. Alas, she was serious. Once outside, she went around to the shed and dragged out the low-riding, red and yellow trike with thick, black tires, otherwise known as a Big Wheel. By this time, my little brother, Junior, was born. My stepbrothers were back in Austin with their mother so it was just my mother, Sofie, Ani, Junior and I taking turns on the one trike. While one person was riding, a couple of us would push and the others would run alongside the trike as we raced up and down the hill our house sat upon.

Standing at the bottom of the hill with my arms raised halfway so that the winner could tag my hand, I watched our precious family having genuine and clean fun. We laughed, we pushed, and we smiled. I watched our beautiful mother running back and forth with us; all the while cheering for us.

As I stood down at the base of the hill I listened to my mother's wide, open-mouthed laughter. The sand was sticking to her teeth like a light brown veil but she wouldn't be disheartened, she simply spat it out and kept on pushing and playing.

Then it was her time to ride and the poor little trike just couldn't bear another load. She sat down and we got behind her to push as she headed down the hill. The Big Wheel broke in the mid-section and exposed her rear end to the rocky, dirt road, and because we had pushed so hard, there was no way we could stop her. Sofie and I went silent and held our breath because we were certain that we were going to be in trouble. When my mother finally collapsed at the base of the hill, she laid out flat on the ground and laughed, so we joined her. We all laughed until the pain in our sides wouldn't allow even the slightest giggle. My heart still smiles as I recall the good times.

On Reading

In the beginning, I read because I loved to read, but later I read because I had to. Reading allowed me to escape the brutal reality that existed in our home. In books I found refuge. In books, I was allowed to be among princes and princesses, in a world where there was plenty of food, bills were always paid and people spoke to one another with kind words in lovely tones. In books, I learned of faraway places, adventurous jobs, and the mysteries of the world like the Bermuda Triangle, Stonehenge, Easter Island and the Pyramids of Egypt. *Estaba buscanda la historia más dulce:* I was looking for the sweetest story.

Luckily, I learned to read quickly and well so my teachers allowed me to take home my reader and books from the classroom library. My mother continued in her tradition of allowing us to choose books from garage sales. She never really censored what I read, so often times I was reading books that were probably inappropriate for me to read. I can only recall one instance in which my mother took a book away from me. I'm not certain, but I believe the book was *The Valley of the Dolls*. She happened to glance over my shoulder as I was reading and saw words like "F***" and "S***" as the author described some pretty graphic sex scenes. She immediately yanked the book out of my hand and asked me why I was reading such trash. She demanded to know where the heck I had gotten such a book. I fearfully responded by saying that it was the only book I had left that I hadn't read and that it was the book she bought for me at the garage sale. Her face turned red with anger and she slapped me upside the head with the book and informed me that it was inappropriate for a nine-year old to be reading such trash. As she walked away, she mumbled something about me not being old enough to handle the content.

A couple of days later, my mother sat me down and had a very serious conversation with me. She told me that she had been thinking about the book and had in fact read the book. She added that she was going to let me have the book back because, basically, she didn't believe in censorship. She wanted me to understand, however, that a reader must take knowledge from books and reflect on what they have read. "Just because it's in a book doesn't mean that you have permission to talk that way or act that way. But at least you'll have a different way to see the world." Further, she said she felt that I was very mature for my age and that I probably could handle that book or any other book for that matter. She said she was proud of me for reading so much and that she hoped I would always have such a passion. What neither she nor I knew then was that reading would one day save my life.

Employed

At the age of nine, I was already spending my summers working in the cotton fields from sunup to sundown. The days always started too early with the necessary preparations of filling the jugs with water, making tortillas, packing *lonches* (lunches) and dressing the younger children so that they would be ready for the long hot days they would be spending waiting in the camper of the truck as we worked the days away. Even though I was often exhausted, I was very proud that I could contribute money to help buy food, and sometimes even fruit.

Working in the fields hoeing cotton is a mindless yet laborious job. The rows seem to go on for eternity and the weeds are sometimes so thick that they can actually break the hoe. The merciless sun burns through your long-sleeved shirt and reminds you of its power. Every once in awhile, a welcomed burst of wind will come rolling through and gently, yet very temporarily, cool your brow.

Sofie was initially allowed to stay in the car while the rest of us hoed our way down the rows and back again. Unfortunately, Sofie found it necessary to eat all of the bean and potato tacos before we got back. The first time it happened, my mother beat the hell out of her with a cotton stalk. The second time it happened, Sofie said she didn't care if she got hit because she was hungry, and then she stupidly added, "Besides it doesn't hurt!"

As soon as I heard that, I took off running to hide underneath the truck because I knew the wrath of my mother was soon to be upon us. And, believe me when I say that my mother's wrath was completely non-discriminating. It is safe to say that Sofie never ate the *lonches* again. And besides, it wasn't long before her stubborn, big-mouthed self had to start working in the fields right beside me.

Working in the fields taught me many lifelong lessons. I learned firsthand about exploitative work and pay conditions, living in the perpetual state of poverty, food insecurity, homelessness, death, injury, illness, exposure to pesticides, and the lack of adequate healthcare.

Work conditions being what they were, I would often find myself daydreaming and convincing myself that surely I had been switched at the hospital and that one day soon my real parents were going to come and rescue me. In my daydreams, my real family lived in a big, air-conditioned home with a swimming pool in the backyard. In that home, I never had to make a single tortilla or hang clothes on the clothesline because they had an indoor washer and dryer. Heck, in that house, we always had running water and electricity, so the heating water for a bath in a little tin tub in our backyard fully exposed to all of creation was one day going to be over.

There I was not responsible for the care and overall supervision of four younger children. I could just imagine how very sad these imaginary parents were without me in their lives. I just so happened to be in that particular frame of mind when the next little scene played out. Of course, it is debatable whether I was daydreaming or simply trying to get out of working so hard. Just the same, here it is. It was a normal, very hot summer day in a cotton field outside of Tahoka, Texas. I was probably around fourteen, working with my grandfather, grandmother, mother, Sofie, Ani and my Tio Felipe I would purposely go as slow as possible in hopes that when the others got to the end of their row, they would turn around and help me with my row. The regular part of the group was on to me, but my Tio Felipe still felt badly for me and would always help me. Now you have to remember that this was back before we had iPods and other types of MP3 players. Walkmans were around but, of course, I didn't have one, so I had to find ways to keep myself entertained on those long days. As we were working our way to the turnaround point, I heard a helicopter overhead. I stopped working, straightened up, leaned on my hoe, took off my hat, and starting looking for it. As I stood there with my hands covering my eyes, I noticed it was a military helicopter. Being unaware of the different branches of the military, I assumed it was an Army helicopter. I attempted to engage my grandfather in a conversation about the helicopter.

"Look, Grandpa. A helicopter. I wonder what you have to do to be able to do that."

No response.

"I want to do that someday."

Everyone started laughing at me. "She wants to be in a helicopter!"

My grandfather gently teased me, "*O sí, mucho de pinche jelihopper. Ponte a trabajar, pendeja.* Basically: "Yeah, right! Sure you're going to ride a helicopter. Get back to work, you idiot!"

I was embarrassed by everyone laughing at me and I asked, "Why can't I ride a helicopter?"

And I translate for you what he responded

to me in Spanish: "God didn't make people like us to ride the helicopters. People like us are made to work. This is the life of the poor."

I was stunned by his response because I had never realized that we were poor nor had I ever conceptualized the fact that I was doomed to live this kind of life *forever*. Didn't everyone live on food stamps? Didn't everyone have grown men doing inappropriate things to them? Wasn't everyone beaten regularly? Surely everyone had to be homeless from time to time or eat out of dumpsters?

As I silently worked the rest of the afternoon mulling over what he had said, I started realizing that I didn't personally know anyone who didn't live the way we did. I started to get behind on my row, but this time I was really sick. I was made nauseous by the dire direction of my life.

My eyes got bigger that day, and my ears sharper. I started watching everything and everyone. I was looking for those who might be different than me. I started listening harder and more purposefully. The types of books I read changed in content. I was desperately seeking the secret of how to be delivered from the life sentence I had been handed.

On God

I can't say for sure why my relationship with Christ was different than it was for anyone else in my family; I only know that I learned at a very early age that I need a lot of Jesus in my life. I vividly recall my mother requiring us to memorize prayers so we could make our First Communion in the Catholic Church. I was very good at memorizing things so I felt a sense of accomplishment at being able to memorize and recite them quickly. I also recall reading the little booklets that the Jehovah Witness people would leave at our door. So that gave me, yet, a different perspective on religion.

My mother or her husband would drop us off at catechism (CCD) classes, and we would learn what we were to memorize. Every now and again we would learn a different Bible story. I was fascinated by the idea that He is an omnipotent, all powerful God, that He can be everywhere all the time, can hear every cry and every whispered prayer. That He is the God of ages. I found refuge in Philippians 2:10-11 that states that one day every knee shall bow and every tongue shall confess onto the name of the Lord.

I would spend hours wandering through the cotton fields pondering His being. I thought of Him as my friend and would find myself talking to Him and playing with Him as if He were with me. Yes, sometimes we'd argue and I would give Him the silent treatment. Sometimes, I purposefully would not look at His beauty. I refused to acknowledge the blue skies, the fluffy clouds, the green trees, the magnificent sunsets or the star-filled evenings. But darn it, He always got me with the scent of wet soil after His precious rains washed the South Plains.

I was then and have always been so in love with Him. So, it was no wonder that I was ecstatic when our CCD teacher informed us that the two people that best memorized their prayers were going to be selected to be Joseph and Mary in a little Christmas play. I knew I was a shoo-in because no one could recite their prayers as well and as quickly as I could. I felt so honored when she called my name. When I got home and told my mom, she was very happy for me and reminded me how very prestigious such a role was—being the mother of God and all! Yikes; I hadn't really thought it through. Even though she was several months pregnant again, this time with twins, she quickly got about the business of making my little costume and telling us how much God meant to her and how she wished she could be there to see me.

It was then that I realized my mother was never happy when she went to church, so I asked her why. She said that if I was old enough to be the mother of God then I was old enough to understand why she could never take communion. She informed me that she was not allowed to take communion because she was a sinner in the eyes of God. Not only because she had disgraced her family by having children outside of marriage with four different men, but also because she had not married in the Catholic Church. I asked her if she still loved God and she said of course she did, and that she was simply getting what she deserved and she had no room to complain.

On the morning I was to play Mary at church, I woke up early and realized that once again my mother's husband had not returned home. He had gotten into the habit of staying out drinking all night and spending what little money we had. He had no regard for the fact that he had left my very pregnant mother at home with four mouths to feed, no groceries, no phone, no money and no car. Luckily, at that time we were living inside the city limits of O'Donnell, Texas, so we were able to walk to school and, on that particular morning, I was to walk to church. I left early because the church was on the outskirts of town, so my walk was going to be a good three miles. Before I left, I told Sofie that she should stay behind and help my mom with the little ones, Ani and Junior, because Junior was still in diapers and my mother shouldn't be lifting him.

The play was disappointingly uneventful and as soon as it was over, I quickly started making my way home. Luckily, one of my aunts saw me walking and gave me a ride home. When she pulled up to our house, I noticed my mother's husband's car was there and that the curtains in the window had all been drawn. I instantly got nervous, knowing this wasn't a good sign. I mumbled a thank you to my aunt and rushed inside. The second I got to the door, I could hear the screaming. I walked in and noticed Junior in his walker and Ani crying in the corner. Sofie just stared at me with terror in her eyes because she didn't know what to do. I pulled off the Mary scarf and ran to grab Junior. I told Sofie to bring Ani and we hid them in the closet. We pretended that it was a game and that we were going to have a tea party.

We put a few plastic dishes and a little tea pot in the closet and before I shut the door, I hugged and kissed Ani and told her not to cry and that it was going to be ok. My poor, sweet, Ani. She never got acclimated to the yelling and the screaming and the violence. It is no wonder the child had bleeding ulcers before she was even old enough to go to school.

Upon shutting the door, I told Sofie to stand guard. I ran back to the living room where my mother and her husband were. She was blocking the front door so that he couldn't leave. Somewhere in their scuffle she had managed to tear off his shirt and exposed the fact that his neck and chest were filled with hickies from the woman with whom he had spent the night. He asked her again to move and she said she wouldn't until he left her with some money to buy milk. I begged her to just let him go, but it was too late. He punched her in the stomach and as she crumpled to the ground, he kicked her on the side and pulled the door open. I saw blood on the carpet beneath her as she grabbed her pregnant belly. With what little breath she had, she asked me to go get help. I ran out the door. I couldn't see, I couldn't think and I had no idea what to do. I ran to the neighbor's house and asked if I could please use their phone because my mom and her husband had been fighting and she was hurt. With calloused eyes and no remorse, my neighbor said, "No, you can't. They're always fighting." With that she slammed the door and walked away. In my craze, I just ran. I went around the corner and saw a house I had never seen and I knocked violently on the door. A woman with gray hair, and glasses over the kindest eyes answered the door. I asked if I could please use her phone and she calmly said yes. She actually called the ambulance herself and turned to me and said, "Help is on the way." With that, I turned around and ran back home. I realized I had no idea who that woman was and I had never seen that house before. Later when I wanted to go back to thank her, I was never able to relocate the house.

The ambulance came promptly and whisked my mother away. In those days, Child Protective Services weren't what they are today, and no one asked a single question regarding our well-being. My mother didn't come home for several days, so I knew not to go to school and not to answer the door. My job was to take care of the kids. It wasn't until the second day that I learned through one of my aunts who had come by the house that the trauma my mother had undergone had caused her to go into labor and that she had given premature birth to my brother and sister, Steven and Angie Lee. Lynn County Hospital just wasn't equipped enough to handle such a delicate situation, and my brother and sister died.

Since my mother was still in the hospital, her husband was responsible for all of the funeral arrangements and he assisted in the digging of the grave. No one ever thought to come by and check on the four of us at home, nor did they think that we needed to attend the funeral. When my mother was released from the hospital, she was very quiet and very skinny. She wouldn't eat or speak. She would wander off to the cemetery and sit by the children's gravesite until the sun came down. Once home, she would sit in her room and listen to her Lee Greenwood songs over and over again. During that time, she never had one single visitor. And I would pray, "Please God, please help my mother. I promise to be good if you will please help her."

With nowhere to turn, she forgave him. He came back and said he had found work and we were moving to Tahoka, Texas. We moved during my fifth grade year. And it was that year that I learned about religion at the Church of Christ. The local Church of Christ had a van that went around picking up the Mexican kids for church as part of their ministry. I felt so lucky to hop on that van! Kyndle Wright was our van driver. She was always happy and sang fun tunes with us such as "Do Lord, Oh, Do Lord, Oh, Do Remember Me." She even taught us a song that helped me remember all the books of the New Testament. I looked forward to Sundays and Wednesdays. It was at that Church of Christ that I met Jewel Parker. She and her husband owned the local pharmacy, Dayton's, but I had never spoken to her. Jewel had two daughters close in age to Sofie and me, so she included us in many activities. She was a mighty woman of God, and I am guessing that was the source of her courage. She was the only person I knew who wasn't afraid of my mother's husband. She would stop by and visit my mother. She spoke gently to my mother and offered to study the Bible with her since my mother was dead set against going to the church. Our relationship with the Parkers grew over the years even though we moved in and out of Tahoka many times as we followed work in our regular migratory circuit. I looked forward to the time of year that we would return to Tahoka because I knew she would be there to welcome us with open arms.

In 1980, my youngest sister was born. So, now my mother had five children and a husband that was only there when he wanted to be. I am thankful for people like Jewel Parker and Glo Hays, also from the Church of Christ, for loving us enough to invite us to their church and attempting to keep us connected to Christ through modeling kindness. One summer, Jewel even talked my mother into allowing Sofie and me to go to church camp. That summer, Glo Hays taught me how to swim. I appreciated the way Jewel dignified us by allowing us to work for the camp fee rather than just giving it to us, it made me feel that much prouder and willing to participate in the activities, knowing I wasn't just some charity case.

In addition to those individuals mentioned above, I have had the blessed opportunity to have some very strong spiritual mentors and role models. Some of those relationships have been in human form and some were found just through readings. Now, I am certain that the ones I know in person didn't realize that I was watching and learning from them, but indeed I was. Those individuals are James V. Baker, JoAnn Newman, Stace McEwin and Vivian McAfee. All of these people have been monumentally instrumental in the growth of my personal relationship with Christ. In my adult life, they are the ones that have taught me of a loving, forgiving and merciful God. They have not only instructed me on the true meaning of grace and humility, but they have walked my journey with me. It is to this team of prayer warriors that I can turn when I am in need of guidance and reassurance. They have encouraged me to always seek to know Him better and grow closer to Him. As Jo always says, "Remember that your testimony is ever changing." How very right she is. Every year it has changed, and every year I learn a little more of His mightiness. I am amazed by the work He has done and continues to do through me as I wait in joyful anticipation of the day I will be with Him.

Before I go any further, however, allow me to tell you of another person that had a life-changing impact on me. In 1969, the year I was born, Maya Angelou wrote a book entitled *I Know Why the Caged Bird Sings*. I happened to come across the book at a yard sale around the age of nine or ten and it is no exaggeration to say that the words in that book worked a miracle in my life. In Chapter 12 of that book, the reader learns of how young Maya was raped by her stepfather and how she survived such a horrid event. I read it, I reread it, and I memorized it.

Now fast-forward. Once again, my mother and her husband were fighting. But things were different now because we had all learned to stay out of the way. It is bizarre how children in such homes learn to survive and go about their business. I was always listening to make sure that along the way he wouldn't kill her. By eleven, I was particularly fearful because he had learned that if he beat her badly enough to be hospitalized, then he would have free reign with her girls. I could tell by the duration of this fight that it was going to be one of those situations. As the ambulance came and carried my mother away, I noticed him glaring right at me. Being the oldest, I always felt a certain sense of responsibility for my siblings, and I knew I was to do whatever I needed to do to protect my younger siblings. And although I was quite aware that I was not able to keep him from getting to Sofie, I still tried. I asked Sofie to take the kids to play, and I went to the back room. The back room was a temporary shed that he liked to take us to because he had become fascinated with taking Polaroid pictures of us in some very distasteful and inappropriate poses. Without going into grand detail, I remember lying on the floor of that room just letting him do his thing because there was no sense in trying to fight him. I kept looking toward the door, so afraid that my siblings would come walking in. And as I was looking toward the door, I saw just the slightest sliver of light coming in from underneath. I remember holding my breath and everything went silent. In my mind's eye, I could see Maya's words: "The child gives because the body can and the mind of the violator cannot," and in that moment I knew with everything in me, that GOD IS GOOD! I felt Him telling me that I would get up off that floor, and that my life had meaning and that I would live a life of purpose.

When my mother's husband was done with me, I stood up and straightened out my little green and white cotton dress, pulled back my long brown hair, looked him straight in the eye and said in a very low but firm voice, "You will *never* touch me again. If you even try, I *will* tell!" I don't know how an eleven-year-old scares the heck out of a grown man, but I could tell by the look on his face that he knew I meant business.

With that, I turned my back on him, something I had never been brave enough to do before, and I went to look for my little sisters and my brother so I could make dinner for them.

Absolutely, my God is GOOD!

[AUTHOR'S NOTE: On October 28, 2010, through the kindness and selfless efforts of my precious friend, Consuelo Castillo-Kickbusch and the legendary Dr. Johnetta B. Cole, I was provided the amazing opportunity to meet Dr. Maya Angelou. During a private conversation with Dr. Angelou, I was able to explain how her book had given me another breath and the permission to be free. Many beautiful things were shared in those special moments and we both understood that we were connected "alma a alma," soul to soul. And it is to God that Dr. Angelou gives all the glory!—just as it should be!]

On Education

I wish I could tell you that all the stars aligned and I was able to live happily ever after, but that's just not how life is and it certainly wasn't that way for me. I did manage to keep him away from me, maybe not from my sisters but that's not my story to tell. I went about my business doing what I was supposed to be doing, but as life at home continued to be difficult it started becoming more and more evident at school.

The effects of our migratory lifestyle started taking their toll on my academic career. Whereas as a younger child, I was able to keep up with most of my readings and lessons, things started to get progressively difficult. By the time I was in third grade, I was starting to get behind on mathematics because I had no one at home that could help me understand multiplication much less division facts. Moving from school to school and sometimes in different states, I started missing huge chunks of instruction. Each new school expected that I was to have learned the material at the school I had just left. I don't recall ever staying in a school for an entire academic school year. And although I spoke functional English, as I got older, it was evident that my level of proficiency was starting to suffer. I had very few friends and, since our stay at each school was for such a brief amount of time, I saw no reason to engage in extracurricular activities. I never joined a club nor played in a single organized sport, unless you count the one day that I played basketball but walked off the court and straight home because I didn't know what to do when I got the ball.

Because we were expected to work as long into the season as possible, it was not unusual for me to start school much later than my peers. Absenteeism became even more of a problem as I got older because I was expected to help provide childcare for my younger siblings when they were sick or my mother was in the hospital.

In the beginning, when I didn't have an assignment I would fib and say I had left it at home or that I had forgotten to do it. The truth was that my home life required so much of me, that homework simply wasn't a priority. Because we often had to walk home, I saw no sense in lugging home huge text books that I wasn't going to be able to use. As time went by, the things I was learning at home started surfacing in my behavior at school. At home I learned that if someone has an attitude with you then you have to have a bigger attitude with them. If someone does something you don't like, then you hit them.

It never occurred to me that I could or should let any one of my teachers know what was happening at home. Moving around so much made it impossible to cultivate relationships strong enough to warrant my trust. I had no real friends and for the most part, my teachers tended to view me as a burden. They knew I would be moving again soon, so they saw very little reason to invest much time in my educational attainment.

Since my mother's marriage was in constant on-again-off-again mode, she started finding companionship with other men in the small towns we lived in, and sometimes those men were the fathers of my peers. Now, I am not just blaming my mom because their fathers had a role in it too, but at the time those children were brutal. The students and sometimes the teachers would have plenty of choice words for us. They spoke viciously about the fact that everywhere I went, I would have four little ducklings behind me. They would tease me and ask if I was sure I wasn't the mother. They would make fun of the fact that we were on food stamps, lived in a dump, and wore stupid clothes. And Sofie's little habit of letting things slide right out of her mouth caused us to have more than a few fights at school.

Yes, the school officials tried everything they knew to do to try to keep us from starting fights. So we got paddled with the board and were sent to In-School Suspension (ISS) and even got expelled from time to time. What did we care? Nothing seemed to dissuade us from our behavior.

One day after being swatted for a lunch time brawl, I returned to my English class to find my teacher, Mrs. Scott, waiting for me. She was about four foot eleven and always wore heels. She looked at me shook her head and said, "Ms. Lisa, I know you're better than this and you are definitely smarter than this, but if you keep this up you are going to get kicked out of Junior Great Books."

It wasn't but a few short weeks later that I really blew it. I was sitting in the school cafeteria and you could tell there was a buzz in the air. You know: all the students know there is going to be a fight and all the adults are clueless. So there I was about to enjoy my delicious pizza and corn entrée when someone tapped me on the shoulder and said, "It's your sister, Sofie. She's about to have a throw down with Gina outside under the big tree!"

I ate a big bite of pizza and couple of spoonfuls of corn and headed to the big tree. There they were—squared off, with all one hundred kids in the district looking on. I inserted a huge Blow Pop lollipop into my mouth and made my way to the front of the crowd. I wanted to have a front row view of this fight. Who wouldn't? Sofie's mean and she's tough and she can put a good beating on the best of them, including me. This is how it went:

Gina: We all know you're nothing but a B****.

Sofie: I know you are but what am I? **[Dang that Pee Wee Herman!]**

Gina: You're going to be a messed up B****

Sofie: Ok, then it's on— tonight. Tonight at the football game underneath the stands.

Random Idiot, aka Me - (*disappointedly*) What? I thought I was going to see some action!

Gina then turned toward me and very confidently said, "Yo Momma!" My eyes got wider as she walked towards me. What was I thinking? Gina towered over my little five-foot-nothing self. I slowly took the Blow Pop out of my mouth as she let her purse slide to the floor. I turned the rings on my fingers because I knew that I had the chance to get in one good hit, and it better count because if she got a good one on me, I was going to be toast. I closed my eyes, and let it rip. I swung at her and hit her right in the nose and blood started spewing everywhere. I jumped on her and wrapped my scrawny legs around her and we landed on the ground. Luckily, the style then was painted-on jeans, so Gina had very little opportunity to get up, even if she had wanted to because her jeans were too tight.

The onlookers were shouting and I heard someone say, "Here he comes!" Out of the corner of my eye, I could see the tall, bald figure of our principal in his sky-blue polyester suit. His long legs stretched as he quickly reached us and attempted to separate the fight. He tried to pry me off of her, but all I kept thinking was that if she got up off that ground she was going to kill me. He pulled us up and stepped between us, but I was too enraged and blinded to realize what was happening. And then it happened. I swung with all my might and hit him with a swift uppercut to the jaw. Everyone gasped, and the crowd separated. The ambulance came for Gina and the principal dragged me and my sister to the office.

I knew by the silence, that this time was different. No one was talking to us. No one said a word. Finally, he showed back up in his office where Sofie and I were seated. He dialed my mother's number and he started to explain what had happened and how that kind of behavior was unacceptable in a school environment. I guess she asked for me because I heard him say, "Yes, ma'am here she is," as he handed the phone to me. He watched me as I put the phone to my ear. And even to this day, I am amazed by what she said, because here I was in serious trouble at school for hurting a girl and assaulting the principal, and, in Spanish she asked me "So, did you win? Because if you didn't, I'm going to kick your ass when you get home!"

It was right then and there that I realized how very different the expectations were for me in my world. On one hand, I had people at the school telling me about appropriate behavior and academic expectations and on the other hand, I had my family sending me a diametrically opposed message. I knew that I needed to be able to figure out how to navigate survival in two entirely different worlds—school and home.

When I returned the phone to the principal, he told my mother to come to the school house and pick us up, and that he would have the paperwork ready when she arrived. We didn't have a car so it took a while for her to arrive. He requested the office aide to clean out our lockers and bring down our personal items while we waited. Sofie and I just glanced at each other. We had no idea what was going on. When my mother arrived, he got right to the point. He informed her in no uncertain terms, that his school had no room for people of our kind. He let her know that because all of his other attempts to change our behavior had failed, we were being kicked out of the district and that we were not to return. As he showed us the door and we slowly filed past him, he pointed right at me and said, "And this one, right here. She'll be barefoot and pregnant before she's 16."

I gasped at his prediction. How dare he! I looked at my mother as I curled my fist, but she said nothing. She just put down her head and started walking home. During that walk, she led the way with Sofie right behind her and me trailing at a distance. I knew she was ashamed, and I was keenly aware that I was the source.

Small Girl, Big School, Wrong Answer

Since we were no longer to attend school in that district, she reconciled with her husband and we moved again. This time we moved to Arlington, Texas. The last thing you want to do with a problem child is move them to a place with better opportunities to cause bigger problems. Within a week, I quickly learned who was dealing what, when, and where. At school, we were taught to Just Say No at home I was taught to Grow and Roll. I got hands-on instruction in the skills of weights and measurements! It was not uncommon to see marijuana in our home. Unfortunately, my mother had gotten into the habit of lighting up with her husband and my stepbrother Anthony on a frequent basis.

I started to hang out with some pretty shady characters. I was doing things I shouldn't have been doing and taking risks I never would have taken before. My poor Algebra I teacher was in shock when she asked me for my homework one day and I marched up to her and emptied my backpack on her desk. The only thing that was in my backpack was the shredded remains of what had once been my Algebra book. I had gotten so frustrated with not understanding what to do and no one to help me, that I decided my actions would keep her from embarrassing me in front of the class every day. I got suspended. And it only got worse from there.

My home life was spinning out of control. One morning, as we were getting ready for school, I could hear them fighting already. Sofie and I were in 8th and 9th grade respectively, so we got the three younger kids dressed and fed and Sofie walked them to school. Just as I walked back into the house to grab my backpack, I saw my mother standing in the living room stark naked. My seventeen year old stepbrother, who had long since dropped out of school, was standing there with a shocked look on his face while his father tried to make my mother put her clothes back on. She kept pushing him away. The next thing I knew, she was running to the back door toward the tool shed. My heart froze. I knew exactly where she was going. She was going to get the gun that we kept hidden in the flooring of the shed. I ran after her but she was too fast. By the time I made it out there, she was already on her way back into the house. She aimed that thing right at him and pulled the trigger. Thank God in Heaven that she is a terrible shot because she let off two more rounds and missed all three times. I don't know if she meant to hurt him or just scare him, but it worked. That man took off quicker than quick; and he was never to live in our home again.

Somewhere in the mix, someone called the police. When they arrived, they asked my mother for the gun and she demurely gave it to them and very cooperatively covered her body with the blanket they offered her. The gun taken, the naked woman covered, and the sorry excuse for a husband and his son running for the hills, all that was left was me. So, the police officer put me in the squad car and drove me to school. He pulled up to the front of the school and dropped me off. Still in a daze, I walked into the front office and the secretary asked if I had an excuse for being tardy. I responded with a quiet, whispered "No." She said, "Well, then, here's your tardy slip. Now get to class because you're late." I walked down the hall to my Physical Science class and the teacher informed me that I needed to hurry because we were about to take a test. Great, I thought. Just what I need. As everyone worked hard on their test, I sat there in utter confusion wondering what the heck had just happened. Was this really my life? Does this teacher really think I care about school?

Be All That You Can Be

Since nothing else seemed to make sense, I talked Sofie into joining me in getting rid of our long, beautiful hair. My mother went ballistic when we walked in with shaved heads. Her physical and emotional dominance over my life had always managed to keep me silent, but inside there was a storm brewing and I was angry. I was angry about having to work at Wendy's during the week and at Trader's Village Flea Market on the weekend. I was angry because there was never enough food, and never enough money. I was angry that she was working herself to the bone, and even then she was skipping meals so that we would have enough to eat. I was angry that her health was going downhill fast. In addition to being angry, I was tired. I was tired of watching the kids. I was tired of cleaning house. I was tired of teachers telling me what to do, and my mother telling me what to do. I was tired of making bad choices and doing things I knew I shouldn't be doing. I was tired of trying to get back on track and trying to get my mother to make better choices because I didn't want to live like that anymore.

So, I did what any right-minded individual that was tired of being told what to do would do: I joined the Army! Surely, no one there tells you what to do!

Of course, they didn't take me the first time I went in to see a recruiter because, after I had completed the practice ASVAB test, I informed the man that I was only fifteen. He just gently laughed and said that even though he admired my desire to serve, I was simply too young. In order to enlist, I needed to be at least seventeen years old. A year and a half later, I was right back in his office and ready to sign on the dotted line. I was in the middle of my Junior year in high school, and since that wasn't working out as well as I had hoped, I had no intentions of returning. My mother was already talking about the next place we would be moving to for work, and I wanted nothing to do with hoeing cotton or pulling onions. When the Army recruiter told me about all the traveling and benefits I would have, I was sold!

Yes, sir, I was proud to be in the U.S. Army Reserves. I was sent to Fort Dix, New Jersey for boot camp and the drill sergeants there certainly got my attention. Now, it wasn't the hollering and screaming and demanding this and that that got to me because I was used to that. (Goodness, didn't they know who my mother was?) It was the fact that all the recruits around me were falling apart. Did there really have to be so much sniffling and boo-hooing? I got such a kick out of the drill instructors coming to scream in their faces. I made the mistake of laughing. Oops! Next thing you know, my short Eddie Murphy look-alike drill sergeant was in my face asking me what I thought was so funny. And that my friends, is how I ended up spending most of my summer in the front leaning rest position (doing push-ups). Yes, I spent many a weekend on latrine detail and kitchen patrol. But other than that, life was fantastic. What was there not to love? For the first time in my life, I was getting three huge meals a day, I had a warm bed all to myself, a safe place to live, the same clothes everyone else was wearing, and they even *paid* me. I thanked God profusely for such a change in my atmosphere. I sent my entire paycheck home to my mother to help her with the kids and I couldn't have been happier.

Yes, there were some physically and

mentally challenging moments but I was up for the task. I worked hard to follow orders so as not to draw attention to myself but my instructor still chose me to be a squad leader. I took the position seriously and truly never horsed around. Throughout my military training, I had several different instructors. I learned more from some than I did from others but that's how it is wherever you go. I really took to heart the notion of being all that I could be. For the first time in life, the playing ground had been leveled and I was learning that I, too, could be successful. I learned that success breeds success and that when you are working as part of the team you are only as strong as your weakest link. There was no way I was going to be that weakest link.

Apparently my superiors noticed my positive attitude, and I was selected to attend different leadership classes and seminars. When I was called in to discuss promotions, I was asked where I was going to go to college. I was immediately concerned because they knew I hadn't finished high school. And what was this college business? I honestly had no idea what college was and I couldn't think of anyone I knew who had gone to college. The sergeant informed me that in order for me to get rank I needed to go back to school.

I left his office thinking that I could just be a Private forever. I didn't mind. I just didn't want him to send me back home. I could work forever with what they were paying me and they would never hear a gripe. Interestingly though, the idea wouldn't leave my mind. I started asking my fellow soldiers where they were going to college. Some of them had even enlisted in order to get money for college. How did I miss that? What was even more dumbfounding was that I knew what total doorknobs some of those people were, so I convinced myself that if they could do it, then I could do it.

I am very appreciative for the military helicopter that flew over the cotton fields that day many years ago because it was that helicopter that planted the seed for me. Joining the military was one of the single most important decisions I ever made. The military opened up doors to opportunities and possibilities that I would never have had otherwise. The military introduced me to a multitude of people that lived in places I had never been and spoke languages of which I'd never heard. I even learned how to use all the different utensils in a formal dinner setting in preparation for an event at which I met President Ronald Reagan. I learned how to hold a conversation with strangers in an appropriate manner without freezing in fear. I learned about discipline, respect, loyalty and mission completion.

All of these skills came in quite handy when I eventually decided to finish high school and go to university. I was reassigned to a Reserve Unit in Lubbock, Texas and was able to attend Texas Tech University. But before I gloss over my days at university, I need to address the fact that my family had a difficult time accepting my decision to go to school. It was difficult for them to understand my desire or necessity to obtain a college education. Unfortunately, it was next to impossible for me to articulate the long-term positive effects of having an education, and I wasn't really sure what they were. I was truly stepping out in faith that God had my every step ordered and that things would work out as they should. One of the bigger problems with me going to school was that I was no longer making an active duty paycheck so I wasn't able to send my mother as much money. I vowed to take another job so I could help with school clothes and school supplies and whatever incidental needs the kids had. So, I went to school full-time, worked as a waitress and still fulfilled my Army Reserve responsibilities. As my educational level went up, my relationship with my family went down. Culturally we had a difficult time agreeing on things. Various family members and old friends started questioning my loyalty to being "Mexicana." They started saying that I was "acting White," that I was a "sell-out," that I was a "wanna-be" and a "coconut." The constant attacks on my desire to go to school made me not want to be around my old friends anymore, and even when we did get together, we had very little we could talk about or do since I had no interest in getting drunk or getting high. One of my mother's friends was especially vicious. She said to me, "You don't need to walk around like your s*** don't stink because everybody knows that a lot of Mexicans start college but they NEVER finish. Soon your ass will be right back here with the rest of us waiting in line for your food stamps."

Now, I'm not going to lie, that woman scared me. Every night when I felt too tired to do my next assignment, I just thought of her gloomy prediction and the fear of it coming true energized me enough to pull countless all-nighters. Not to give her more credit than is due, however, there is actually another huge reason that I was successful in undergrad school—Kappa Delta Chi.

Since you already know about my childhood and my military connections, you can rightly guess that I am not standard sorority girl material, so when my roommate asked me to accompany her to sorority rush you can bet I laughed out loud. I informed her that I was not a "Bow Head" nor was I interested in being in a room full of them. She assured me that I wouldn't have to join. I just needed to go to Rush with her and then she would make friends and I would be off the hook after that. Since she had been so considerate while I had been stationed in South Carolina by getting all of my admissions paperwork taken care of, I felt like I owed her at least that, so I agreed to go.

When I arrived to the meeting room, I was greeted by a woman dressed like Zsa-Zsa Gabor. She spoke to us and introduced us to the other not-so-flamboyant members. I learned that she was Cynthia Garza and among the women with her were Nellie Ledesma, Irene Montoya, and Melissa Montoya, the founding members of Kappa Delta Chi; that they had officially been recognized by the University on April 6, 1987; and that their purpose was to promote the values of Unity, Honesty, Integrity and Leadership among women at colleges and universities. Further, I learned that the foundation of their sorority was built on friendship, service and Christianity.

Even with all that information, I was still a little skeptical. I kept waiting for their kindness to wane but it didn't. At the end of the night, we were informed that we would be contacted if we were going to be invited to join their sorority. I didn't hold my breath since it was my roommate that wanted to join, not me. And wouldn't you know it, they contacted me and not my roommate (the reason she wasn't invited was because she wasn't taking a full course load). Again I laughed and again my roommate talked me into it, saying that she would join the following semester when she was taking a full course load. In the Spring of 1989, I pledged Kappa Delta Chi and have been connected to it ever since.

Being a part of the Sisterhood allowed me the opportunity to engage in my school and my community in a meaningful way. The study hours coupled with a required GPA helped me stay focused on keeping my grades up. The required service hours helped me learn to recognize and address the needs in our community through volunteerism. For once in my life I was able to understand the causes and consequences of community problems and issues. Volunteering taught me skills in collaboration and coordination and instilled in me a sense of compassion for others.

Because my relationship with Christ was so important to me, I felt especially blessed that Nellie and Cynthia were my pledge trainers (aka new member educators) because they absolutely modeled and impressed upon us the loving ways of Christ. Every meeting started and ended in prayer and they even scheduled separate Bible study times for all that were interested. My love for KD CHI only grew and my commitment increased as we endeavored to expand our organization into other universities throughout the country. I was serving as the KD CHI's first National President when we expanded to Texas A&M and the University of Texas in El Paso. Today, with chapters located nationwide, KD CHI continues to serve Hispanic communities and is recognized as having one of the strongest networks of Latina leaders in the country.

I took to heart the quote, "Our life is God's gift to us, what we do with it is our gift to God," and I can't explain how wonderful it feels to belong to a sisterhood of women that feel the same way. Our sisterhood is populated with strong women from every walk of life. We come from different ethnicities, races, cities, countries, religious beliefs, and economic backgrounds. Our educational aspirations and interests vary and we come in all shapes and sizes but we are all beautiful. Our beauty comes from the things we do agree upon—leading with integrity and remaining united through service.

To this day, some of my most profound and enduring friendships are with my KD CHI sisters. My children are blessed to have so many fabulous, hard-working, spiritually centered aunts. So yes, the military got me to school, but it was definitely Kappa Delta Chi that kept me there.

In 1992, I received a Bachelor of Arts degree from Texas Tech University. I immediately sought employment as an educator. My mother-in-law informed me that Tahoka Independent School District was seeking a high school English teacher. I had never bothered to let her know that I had been expelled from that district several years before, and I suspected if the district didn't want me to attend their school as a student they certainly wouldn't want me teaching their students. (Actually, I had briefly returned to the district a year or two after being expelled, during which time I was selected to be the school mascot. Thanks to Patti Rambo for sticking up for me and Joan Knox for keeping me.) When I learned there was a new principal, I figured it might be safe to apply: after all I had changed and I had a different last name.

When I got there, I asked for an application and the receptionist handed me one for the custodial position. When I looked at it, I asked her if I had the right application because I was seeking to obtain the teaching position. She quickly grabbed it from me and tsked as she said with a smirk, "Honey, you need a degree for that." Still a little confused, I asked, "Is it okay if I get it on Saturday? That's when I graduate." She was obviously embarrassed by the situation and quickly and sincerely apologized. Just then the principal walked into the office. He interviewed me and walked me down to the classroom where I would be teaching. Since it was a mid-year position and winter holidays were right around the corner, the students were exceptionally hyper and disengaged with the lesson being taught. They were sitting on the desk tops, spitting paper wads, and appeared completely uninterested in meeting a new teacher.

The principal looked at me and asked me if I thought I could handle them. Having recently been on Active Duty with the military, I confidently responded, "Yes, sir. Not only can I handle them, they're going to learn something!"

As we were walking back to the office, he informed me that a decision would be made soon and that perhaps I should meet the Superintendent. "Oh, look. Here he is," he said. And wouldn't you know it, the Superintendent was the very principal that had been forced to expel me all those years ago. *Great*, I thought, *I am so unemployed.*

He shook my hand and kept looking at me. "Don't I know you?" he asked. "No, sir," I said trying to sound as convincing as possible while looking at my feet. I had never been so thankful for military bearing. He asked me a couple of questions and the principal gave him additional information on my military experience and educational achievements. The entire time I was holding my breath waiting for the other shoe to drop. Just as he was walking out of the office, he stopped, turned around, looked right at me and said, "I remember you. You were the one we had to take out of here kicking and screaming." Being the good man he is, he saved me the embarrassment of going into the details. He came back in and shook my hand again, this time honestly and earnestly and told me he was happy to see me back and that he was proud of how I had turned things around.

By the time I returned to my apartment that evening, there was a message on my answering machine from the Principal offering me my first teaching position. He was willing to take a risk I think very few in his position would have taken. I was assigned to teach 10th and 11th grade English. At the end of that year, I was assigned to teach 7th and 8th grade Language Arts and English as a Second Language. After a few years there, I moved to teach English and Spanish in a high school located closer to my home in the city where I lived. I continued teaching high school as I completed my Master's Degree and obtained mid-management certification. Upon completion of my Master's, I accepted a position as an assistant principal in an elementary school.

It was in that position, that I met Mr. James V. Baker. He had been asked to come out of retirement to mentor me. What an odd pair we were—he was a tall White man with 36 years of working with elementary aged children, and I was a short, Mexican American woman with a few years of junior high and high school teaching experience sprinkled with prior military experience. A better match could never have been made. I learned so much from him. In the first couple of years, I followed him like a little duckling. I listened. I watched. I learned. One day, I walked into his office and he was reading from a little, tiny, worn-out black Bible. I asked him what he was reading and he shared. He shared that day and for several years, the goodness of our wonderful Lord and Savior. I looked forward to those lessons, but not just in the Word but through application of the Word. He didn't have to preach to anyone at anytime, he was living it. It was evident in his interactions with others, whether they were teachers, parents, students, custodians, or cafeteria workers He loved everyone, he dignified everyone. Yes, he did get frustrated with people but in those times he would remind me that we are all living in the "human predicament" and that as humans we will always disappoint each other. He added that disappointment is natural and that it doesn't have to lead to writing people off. He taught me that you have to trust those you work for and with; but, in order to build trust you need to invest time and energy into establishing relationships. In a conversation regarding trust and his experiences in training pre-service principals to successfully lead schools, he said:

"I think trust requires commitment, love, communication and courage. One of the specific acts in my life related to trust, one thing I've already referred to is working with my partner principals. I had to trust them, and I did. I took them in and said, we're going to be a part of this together. We're going to be co-principals. We're going to work on this. We're going to have lots of conversations. We're going to be very open. We're going to try to be transparent with each other. And we're going to be committed. We're going to care for each other. We're going to communicate with courage and share back and forth. And we're going to try to do this with our staff, kids and parents.

This has been very fulfilling, empowering, and profitable educationally and spiritually to have done this. To help encourage others to lead and develop themselves and to learn how to lead better, myself, by trusting my partners and my staff rather than operating through skepticism and control."

I share this conversation with you because it has impacted the way I have chosen to lead schools and organizations. The experiences I had and the lessons I learned under his tutelage positively influenced the direction of my professional life by clarifying for me that yes, it is necessary that everyone in the school or the organization be working toward the same mission to impact change. I also learned that everyone has to be empowered to be responsible and accountable for their own trustworthiness and contribution to the team—especially the "boss."

After four years as his assistant principal, he practically kicked me out so I could take my own school. I had been asked to take a low-performing school in another district and with his encouragement and support, I left. While in that district, I was provided the wonderful opportunity to take yet another low-performing school that was on the verge of closure. I gladly accepted that challenge and in 2004, we opened the doors to Lubbock Independent School District's first charter campus, the Ramirez Charter School. In that position, I was successful in leading all aspects of the new school, from writing and evaluating grant applications, to establishing community relations and support, to selecting and training a new staff, to building an effective learning community for parents, students and staff.

Working as a principal, I learned that if you really want to make the top level decisions, you have to be the superintendent. So once again, I returned to school. I completed my superintendent certification and started my coursework for a doctoral degree. In 2006, I joined the U.S. Department of Education, where I was appointed group leader for the discretionary grants team, which plans and coordinates the High School Equivalency Program (HEP), College Assistance Migrant Program (CAMP), and the Migrant Education Even Start (MEES) program. In my current role as Director of the Office of Migrant Education, I manage and lead the planning and coordination of all aspects of the Migrant Education Program office, including grant and contract administration, policy, evaluation, and special initiatives. As the director of migrant education in the Office of Elementary and Secondary Education at the U.S. Department of Education, I now have the opportunity to converge my personal and professional experiences to help improve the academic success of migrant students across the country.

In 2009, through the many sacrifices and

continued support of my husband Mike and my precious children, I was able to complete my Doctor of Education (Ed.D.) degree in Educational Leadership from Texas Tech University. Additionally, I can proudly say that I am an alumna of an Executive Leadership program at the John F. Kennedy School of Government at Harvard University. Now tell me God can't use broken vessels! It is in Him that we can be all that we were called to be. To Him be all the glory!

part two

Reflections

Through reflection on the experiences you read about in the Part I of this book along with many others that didn't make it into this volume, I have been able to extricate some significant lessons for the direction and development of my life. These pearls of wisdom have served me through all the stages and phases of my life, both in personal and professional respects. The lessons that I have learned are in the areas of

1. Compassion
2. Competency
3. Choice + Choice Formula

4. Spirituality in Educational Leadership

As I speak around the country, I have enjoyed having conversations with a variety of different stakeholders regarding these four areas. I always start those conversations with a disclaimer because as you can probably tell, I prefer to put everything out on the table. I make the audience aware that many toes will get stepped on and some beliefs are going to be challenged. And it's not to say that my point of view is right and theirs is wrong, it's just **different**! The bottom line is that as educators we are tasked to educate, not judge. We don't have to agree with or accept the way a family unit is managed. Nor do we have permission to negatively script a student based on our own stereotypes, myths or beliefs about others that are different than we are. Of course, we have an obligation to report anything that may be endangering the child or others in the home, and yes, we must consider the whole child's well-being including physical and mental health along with other basic needs and considerations. But at the end of day, as educators, we must stay focused on the fact that our job is to educate. People, in general, are not comfortable with being asked to step out of their comfort zone but I have learned that most educators want to do an excellent job and they take their profession very seriously. Most educators want to be challenged to learn different ways to reach the hardest to reach students. They want their lives and their professional contributions to be meaningful. I won't deny that there are exceptions to the rule and those individuals should not be allowed to continue failing our students, but I'll discuss that in the Competency chapter of Part II.

It is interesting how differently parents view these areas when compared to the views of teachers and students. I have come to recognize that the thoughtful contributions of high school students with respect to how these areas affect their lives is often dismissed or devalued, yet they are the ones responsible for implementing the plan for their educational career. The benefits of placing time and effort into building relationships with all members of the school community, including the students themselves, should never be underestimated.

Compassion

He who oppresses the poor shows contempt for their Maker, but whoever is kind to the needy honors God.

Proverbs 14:31

When I was in fourth grade, I learned two invaluable lessons. The first lesson conveyed to me the true meaning of compassion. Compassion is a deep awareness of the suffering of another coupled with the wish to relieve it. To me, compassion is not the same as empathy or sympathy. From my personal experience, empathy is extremely difficult to achieve because you can never really experience what another is experiencing if you haven't been there. And I never really liked the idea of sympathy because it always felt like people pitied me, and I didn't and still don't want people to feel sorry for me. Charity is just as bad because too often there is this sense that the recipient is then indebted to the giver. For obvious reasons, I have never enjoyed the feeling of indebtedness and am a firm believer that one should not strive to repay a kindness to the giver but rather spread the kindness by adhering to the notion of Paying it Forward.

The story I am about to describe was the first instance in which someone outside of my family had taken an interest in my home situation and then paired it with an action that served to relieve some of the pain of embarrassment. For many years prior to and after fourth grade, I was subjected to and tolerated unjust treatment from many strangers including that of school personnel. Whether it was witnessing the secretary that spoke to my mother in a long, slow, degrading, drawn-out, and very loud voice because she assumed that since my mother primarily spoke Spanish that she must be dumb; or the rude and insensitive remarks a teacher I met at church made when she asked me whether or not I was certain that Sofie and I weren't just "nine months apart" (snicker, snicker), I felt I had no choice but to take it in silently, and respectfully.

The year of 1979 brought me an angel by the name of Ms. Jimmie Pace. Ms. Pace was the migrant education teacher at the school I attended in Lamesa, Texas. Every afternoon, the principal would come over the loud speaker and say, "Pardon this interruption, it is now time for the Mexican kids to report to the portables." I welcomed that announcement and would quickly gather my things and head to the portable where her classroom was housed. I was a quirky, skinny, little girl that dressed in my stepbrothers' hand-me-downs. I had horrible teeth, bad skin, ridiculous eyeglasses and super thick hair that I kept braided, as was the tradition and expectation for Mexican girls at the time. Ms. Pace, on the other hand was a larger, beautiful woman with snazzy, short, dark hair, big, glassy eyes, and perfect makeup. She always carried a delicate yet captivating scent of perfume. On top of all that, she was kind to me. She took a genuine interest in me and my family. She was the first teacher I had that wasn't afraid to sit right next to me when she spoke to me and to give me a daily hug. She would squeeze just tight enough and remark, "Gee, your hair smells terrific!" That would always make me laugh because that was the name of the shampoo I used.

As many schools as I had attended, and there were many, as we moved several times a year, she was the only teacher I ever had that invited my mother to Open House. When she first asked, I was embarrassed to tell her that my mother probably wouldn't come because she didn't feel comfortable at schools and was a little nervous about speaking English. Ms. Pace responded by waving me off after she handed me an envelope addressed to my mother. I proudly took it home and showed it to my mother who was quite pleased that she had received a personal invitation. I quickly promised that I would get all my chores done the night before if she would please attend my Open House. I told her all about Ms. Pace and assured her that as soon as she met Ms. Pace we could go home. Wonder of all wonders, my mother did attend. And that evening was surreal to me. There we were, the three of us—my favorite teacher, my precious mother, and me. Ms. Pace told my mother how smart and polite I was and my mother just beamed. She was so proud. Ms. Pace didn't spend a lot of time with us because she had to interact with the other students as well. But that didn't matter, it had been just enough time for her to smile profusely and genuinely to my mother and my mother felt it—I felt it. I think this is an important lesson because something I've learned firsthand through my work with children is that children love their mothers. No matter what the situation is, no matter how horrible we tend to think her parenting skills may be, children want their mother's approval and acceptance. Mothers are often a child's first teacher and biggest

Dulcified   93

influence, it behooves us as educators to withhold judgment on a child's mother (and/or father) and choose to work in concert with them to benefit the children we are responsible for teaching. I shall never forget how Ms. Pace dignified my mother and treated her like a special human being.

Twenty years later, Ms. Pace and I met again. It was at the AIM High event in Lamesa, Texas, that I mentioned in the first part of this book. When she and I finally met up again after all those years and I had the opportunity to tell of the impact her act of compassion had had on me, she was sad. She was sad because she couldn't remember me. She thought that I would be disappointed because she had forgotten me. On the contrary, I couldn't have been happier because that meant that she treated everyone that way—and that alone spoke volumes to me about the goodness of her character. Through the years, she and I have kept in contact. Since that time, she has battled and survived breast cancer and numerous other life tragedies, but she is forever optimistic and kind. She was even there for me when I received my doctoral degree thirty years after she was my fourth grade teacher. Talk about making a difference!

Have you thanked an individual that has made a difference in your life? If you haven't, please consider sending him/her a little message of gratitude by way of a thank-you note. Your kindness will not go unnoticed.

Competency

Not that we are competent in ourselves to claim anything for ourselves, but our competence comes from God.

2 Corinthians 3:5

The second invaluable lesson I learned in fourth grade was a lesson in competency. My fourth grade math teacher used to reward all individuals that could complete a worksheet on their multiplication math facts in less than three minutes with a 3 Musketeers candy bar. If I could beat the timer, I would have the entire candy bar to myself. I wouldn't have to share with anyone. I could take big, fat bites and no one would be able to say a thing because it would be mine—all mine. Unfortunately, every time I tried to beat the timer, I just couldn't do it. There would always be at least three questions left unanswered. Even though I was showing vast improvement, I wasn't making the mark.

One afternoon, I showed up in her classroom with withdrawal papers because once again it was time for us to follow the crops. As I handed her my forms for her signature, she asked me if I had received my candy bar. I let her know that I had not yet been able to beat the timer. "Well," she said, "let's try one more time." I hesitated because I knew my mother was waiting for me in the car but I really wanted the candy bar so I sat down. She pulled out a fresh worksheet, two sharpened pencils, and set the little egg timer and the candy bar right on my desk. Once she started the timer, I started flying through the questions. One after the other, the answers were coming to me. I was going to do it this time. This time, I was going to walk away with that candy bar!

BUZZZZ! The timer went off and my teacher came over to my desk to review my worksheet. "Oh, Lisa, it looks like you still had one more question to answer."

What do you think happened? Do you think I got the candy bar? After all, there I was all sad and pitiful looking and I was moving to the next town. Hey, I had shown great improvement, she said so herself. Would you have given me the candy bar?

She looked right at me, smiled, and said, "Well, Lisa, it looks like you will have to keep working on your math facts in your next school. Don't give up, OK? You are a very smart young lady and I know you can do it." With that, she picked up the candy bar and placed it back in her desk.

Heck, no she didn't give me the candy bar. At first, I couldn't believe that she didn't feel sorry for little ol' me. Hey, at least I tried! Was I not pathetic enough for her to give me the darn candy bar? Eventually, I learned to be thankful that she didn't give me the candy bar. I learned a couple of lessons that day. I learned that there is nothing free in the world, you have to work for what you want in the world, and you have to earn it. I also learned that I don't want people to pity me and water down standards and expectations because they feel sorry for me. Just as importantly, I learned that indeed I was very capable of mastering my math facts and anything else I put my mind to—but it would mean that I would have to use my time wisely and align my actions with my goals.

She did nothing wrong, in fact, she did everything right. She exhibited competency. Competency is an interesting word. Competency occurs when one is properly or sufficiently qualified. Therefore, it is possible for one to be certified and not be competent. You can follow a process and properly fulfill the requirements to be an educator and still not be sufficiently prepared enough to actually teach what you know. To teach is to cause to learn. If your students aren't learning, you're not teaching. Certified does not equate to being competent. In the example I shared above, my teacher worked toward adequately preparing me to meet an established and clearly articulated standard. She exhibited excellence in providing me with additional opportunities to meet the standard. At no time was it acceptable to accept less from me or to lower the standard. I have no doubt that if I had stayed with her I would have learned my math facts and so much more. As educators, it is important for us to have ability in the areas we are tasked to teach, understand the high standards by which our students are to be measured, and then adequately prepare our students to meet those standards. In speaking of meeting high standards, it is necessary we understand it is required of the students and teachers alike.

Just because you have a degree and a title it doesn't necessarily mean you are fully aware, prepared or competent. We have to continually challenge ourselves to keep learning and modifying the way we operate in order to adequately prepare our youth for tomorrow's challenges. If you have laminated your lesson plans, you have probably stopped learning some time ago. If the majority of your students are failing your class, you have failed to teach them.

Take some time to reflect on how many times you have "dumbed down" a lesson or statement because you didn't think the person on the receiving end was capable of understanding you. Do not do it out of a misplaced sense of pity. Your students don't need your pity, they need your help and your help comes in the form of an education. They need a strong, solid, global education. You must continue to hold the standard high but you must guide them on how to get there. As educators, we have to remember that we have jobs *because* of our students, not in spite of them. If you are one of those "cool" teachers that allow students to drink Dr. Pepper and eat peanuts in your class as they visit the hours away, stop! If you are the leader in a school where teachers are refusing to do their job, then do *your* job and start addressing the situation. Do not be afraid to have those very necessary conversations. You are in charge, so take charge. Every time you feel hesitant to confront one of those employees, I want you to pick one of your neediest students and imagine yourself telling that child that you are willing to sell them out because you are afraid to do the job you were hired to do. Yes, I have heard the excuse, "They don't pay me enough to do this job." Except in the case of some very unusual circumstance, it's probably the same amount that was on the contract when you signed and accepted the responsibility of being an educator. All I'm asking is that you commit to being competent by being fully aware and prepared. Just do your job and educate.

Choice + Choice
Formula

Do you not know that in a race all the runners run, but only one gets the prize? Run in such a way as to get the prize.

1 Corinthians 9:24

While I was in the military, I learned a very important fact of life—every decision has a consequence. Sometimes the consequence is positive and sometimes the consequence is negative. Granted that there are some situations in which we don't have a choice and things happen to us, but we still get to choose the way we respond. Further, we have a choice in the attitude we bring to any given situation. Since I am a very visual learner, I created a little formula that I have taught to hundreds of students over the years. Of course, when I teach the students, I also teach them the accompanying hand signals that go with the formula. The formula is:

Choice + Choice = The Direction of Your Life

Every single day, we are tasked to make a multitude of decisions. We decide things such as, what time to wake up, whether to press the snooze button or get out of bed, to brush our teeth, not brush our teeth, what to wear, what to eat, where to go, and what to do once we get there. Of course, those are the small choices we make, but those small choices populate every single one of our days. Those days turn into weeks, months and, in time, years. Eventually, we find ourselves wondering where all our time went and we question why we didn't get more accomplished during that time. Worse yet, sometimes we find it easy to start blaming others for our failures—if I had done this, if I had done that, if so-and-so would have done this or that. In the school setting, I would hear, "Miss, it's not my fault, its what's-her-name's fault, she's prejudiced, she hates me, she's out to get me, she just likes the White kids…" When I hear such ranting, I quietly listen and wait until they are done with all their excuses. Then I ask, "What were you responsible for? What were you supposed to do? What about your actions demonstrated that you were doing what you were supposed to be doing?" This always causes people to step back for a minute to think. I then explain that you cannot be responsible for how others act or behave we can only be responsible for the part we bring to the equation. That part is exhibited in every choice we make.

I often give them one of two scenarios. I'll ask them, "If you were making the roadmap of how you are to get to your very successful life, what would it look like?" or "Pretend that you are an actor in a huge motion picture, and you are the main star, how would you like for the movie of your life to play out? "

Whenever possible, I allow them to draw pictures on chart paper and to explain in full detail what they have drawn out. This exercise works well with parents as well because most parents want good things for their children—yes, even the parents that appear to be completely disengaged with their child's education.

Next, we apply the formula: Choice + Choice= The Direction of Your Life. I ask them if they can honestly say that their actions and choices are moving their life in the direction that they just said they wanted. Even though it may seem like a simple, meaningless process, I have seen faces light up with a new awareness of the power of their choices.

Everyone, without exception, should have a very clear image of what their personal mission or purpose is and then he/she must assume responsibility for the choices that are made as they try to get there. To me, the path is very clear: Do it or Don't! I don't have a whole lot of sympathy for excuses. If I am bombarded with lots of excuses, I start working on taking those excuses away. First of all, the person needs to be able to succinctly articulate what the obstacle or challenge (aka excuse) is. Secondly, the individual needs to write down possible solutions. Next, the individual should implement the solution or plan. Finally, they must evaluate to see if the plan/solution gave them the intended result—if so, continue doing it, if not, modify the plan/solution or use a different one. This logic is not mine; I simply adapted a continuous improvement model and modified it to be used in everyday situations.

Without fail, I would encounter students that would say, "But Miss, I can't because my father's a drunk, my mother's on drugs, my family is in a gang, because I have a baby." The list can go on and on—and yes, I recognize that those things can make life very difficult but I cannot accept that those things justify an individual doing nothing about it. I had a poster in my classroom that read:

Don't allow the bad things in your life to be the excuses for why you are not successful, they should be the reason you ARE successful!' If your dad is a drunk, do you really want to keep living like that? If your mom is on drugs, do you want that to be your profession? If you have a baby, don't you think that you will need an education so you can eventually provide the child with a better life?

Even with the best intentions, progress sometimes eludes us, or so it seems. What often happens is that we want to see big changes and we want to see them now. That's just not how it works. Progress is often painfully slow and it is only through very mindful, purposeful steps that we can start to see the pigments that color in our dreams. It's one choice after another because choice plus choice equals the direction of your life.

This afternoon during my run along the trails that lace the Potomac River, something very common yet special happened. I was jogging along with my headphones on and my dog in tow, when I noticed three people riding their bikes in the opposite direction. There was a father, a young boy around five years old, and a little girl around eight years old. The young boy was racing his little blue bike as fast as he could way ahead of his father and sister. Without warning, the boy's tire hit a bump in the road and the child was thrown off his bike and the trail. Since I was running toward him, I was going to speed up a little to help but I noticed that his dad very calmly rode his bike into a safe position off the trail and the little girl followed her dad's lead. He raced over to his son. I could see that the child had cut his knee and his face was covered in tears. I happened to be running right by them as his father reached the child. When I reached up to take off my headphones, I heard the child wailing in pain as his very capable father reached his strong hands underneath the child's arms closest to his armpits and lifted him while saying in a firm but comforting voice, "Stand up."

The incident gave me shivers because that is how I picture our very capable Father in Heaven. When we experience bumps in the road and get scuffed up and even when we endure injuries, He is calm and strong and can give us comfort. He understands even when we don't, that we can stand up—it is we that don't understand nor believe that we can stand. When we are in the midst of our pain, we often don't want to stand. We are lucky sometimes if we can crawl. If that is how you feel, then crawl. I am here to tell you, **crawling is progress**! If you are in a situation that you find unacceptable, then do something about it. You've heard the saying, just put one foot in front of the other; if you need to put one knee in front of the other, then do it.

Spirituality in Educational Leadership

When I returned to Texas Tech University to acquire my superintendent certification, my professor, Dr. Mendez-Morse, invited me to assist with one of her research projects. It was called the Latina Educational Leaders: Resiliency in Leadership Project (Mendez-Morse, 2003).

Working in collaboration with the members of the research project team afforded me invaluable insight into the realm in which resiliency not only exists, but how it is defined in terms of resistance.

Lisa R. Ramírez, Ed.D.

My initial role in the project entailed the discussion of "learning to be resilient"; however, through the natural progression of meaningful interactions with the other participants, I discovered among many recurring themes, my ever-present, strongly felt theme of spirituality.

Because I was the youngest member on that research team, as well as the participant with the least amount of educational leadership experience, I felt compelled to reflect on the events that resulted in my being at the doorstep of such an incredible academic threshold. My personal belief and understanding of how spirituality influenced my life and career continued to nag at me. Initially, I felt that spirituality had no place in the academic realm. However, as my educational leadership career began to mature, I realized through my relationship with my mentor, a spiritually-centered leader, that spirituality most definitively contributed to the formation of my commitment to the advancement of social justice through education. My interest in the role of spirituality in the lives of educational leaders led me to research several different aspects of spirituality, ranging from attempting to define spirituality to what the enactment of spirituality looks like in practice. I soon learned that the literature available contained very limited discourse on the topic, and what little did exist was often muted. It was then that I decided to apply for the doctoral program in hopes of continuing my research and contributing to the presence of literature that describes the role of spirituality in the lives of educational leaders.

During my time in the doctoral program, I conducted an exploratory case study designed to identify the role of spirituality in the work of four public school principals. The study investigated the evidence of spirituality in the principals' work as it related to eight key principles presented in Houston and Sokolow's <u>The Spiritual Dimension of Leadership</u> (2006). In summary, the study advanced the research that identified evidence of leading through spirituality as it relates to previously identified spiritual principles and it documented the effect and meaning of leading through spirituality.

The advancements are important to the educational leadership field for several reasons. First of all, understanding spirituality is critical to the development of many educational leaders especially when it has been identified as a source of strength. Secondly, it is necessary to be able to recognize and to identify spiritual principles and their source, in oneself and others. Thirdly, it clarifies the purpose of cognitively and intentionally choosing to employ the use of a Spiritual Filter (SF) while having a functional understanding of possible effects, positive and/or negative, on educational leadership. Fourthly, the research added to the minimal understanding that exists about the lives of educational leaders that choose to lead through spirituality. Such contribution serves to encourage other researchers to approach this topic in meaningful ways so as to reveal otherwise muted discourses. Lastly, but equally as important, the study illustrated the significance that spirituality and spiritual principles play in the lives of educational leaders. The findings of my research served to improve my own understanding of how resiliency, resistance, and well-defined spiritual principles inform my work and the work of many other educational leaders. In particular, it helped me to discover many in-depth perceptions on the functioning of spiritual principles. Each individual leader has her/his own definition of spirituality, shaping elements of life, lived work experiences as they pertain to these spiritual principles, and meaning for spirituality in their work. I also recognize the connectedness of the perceptions of spiritual leaders pertaining to the right to retain dignity of all human beings. In saying this, I am convinced that awareness and relationship with the self are of great import if educational leaders are to persevere and remain effective.

The struggle to continue as an educational leader often times feels overwhelming, but I know I must stay true to the principles that have not led me astray. The spiritual capital (the spiritual attributes, possessions, and qualities) that I bring with me to my personal and professional roles has a value that I have yet to fully comprehend.

part three

Tying Up Loose Ends

The years of hard work and tough work conditions, along with inadequate access to health care, left both of my grandparents in poor health much sooner than what is commonly expected. My mother, in fulfillment of her sense of obligation to my grandparents, moved to South Texas to care for them. She was one of the primary care providers when my grandfather passed away in 2003. In March of 2011, I received a call from my mother informing me that my grandmother had passed away.

Before I hung up the phone, she told me

that it would be ok if I couldn't make it to the funeral since I was so far away. I informed her immediately that Washington, DC is not located across the universe and that of course I was planning to attend the funeral. It wasn't until I was actually in San Antonio, Texas that I realized what I had done.

For many, many years I have been absent from most of my family events. Because I refused to be silent about my past and because my educational attainment had allowed me to live a very different lifestyle, my family often assumed that I didn't want to be part of their family functions. In all fairness, I am not sure that I demonstrated any behavior that would lead them to believe otherwise. The situation became even more complicated when I started having children, because I absolutely refused to allow my children to be near her husband.

It wasn't until my early twenties that my mother became fully aware of the abuses that had occurred in our home when she wasn't there. Whether she suspected anything is uncertain but it is certain that she knew by the time I was twenty-one. When I finally decided to reveal the past to her, her husband (they are still married even though they have not lived together since she tried to shoot him), decided to tell her first. I am not certain how he told her and I don't know how much he told her. I just know he told her. As soon as she learned, she called me immediately to confirm what he had said. I remember being scared to tell her when I was a child because I was afraid that he would kill her, but as an adult I was fearful that it would break her heart and that she would blame herself. There was no way that I could have prepared myself for what actually happened when she found out. Of course, she was upset and became very silent. I remember allowing her time to process what she had just heard. I excused myself from the call and hung up the phone. I looked at Mike and just gave him a shrug. All we could do was to wait and see how she would take it.

Even though she expressed her anger and disbelief and later she tried to blame herself, she still opted to communicate with him. He was still allowed in her home, she still prepared meals for him and my siblings still interacted with him as if nothing had happened. I felt so betrayed. I could not wrap my mind around how a mother could choose a man over her child. I cannot express the anguish and pain I felt because all those years, I felt like I had protected her and our family and now I felt as if she had abandoned me. To add insult to injury, her husband had the gall to say that I was crazy and that even if all those events *did* happen, it wasn't "that big of a deal." He even had the nerve to tell me that I needed to get closer to God because the Devil was making me say crazy things.

When I sought solidarity with my sister

Sofie, since she had experienced the same abuse, she informed me that she preferred not to discuss it again and asked me to respect her need to handle it in her own way. I agreed to respect her wishes but I informed her that I expected all of them to understand that I would no longer be silent. And silent I wasn't. My relationship with Christ had freed me from my shame. His mercy had delivered me from the shackles of my past and His grace had provided me a life exceedingly and abundantly more blessed than anything I could have ever imagined.

And it was in that mindset that I had lived the majority of my adult life. I was living with the belief that I was free. I worked hard in my personal and professional career to achieve excellence. I vowed to help the marginalized and disenfranchised obtain an education so that they too could break free from the vicious cycle of poverty and all its unintended consequences and side effects. I challenged myself to strive for continuous improvement and to learn from every situation. I wanted my life and the lives of my children to be enriched by meaningful experiences populated with people that loved them and cared for them. I sought honesty, loyalty and integrity in all my relationships both personal and professional. I committed myself in service to children with special needs and their families through our church ministry.

What I couldn't do was the one thing that my friend Jo had warned me would be the hardest thing to do. "Sweet friend," she said, "I learned many years ago that the hardest forgiveness to give is the forgiveness not asked for." And she was right. I had not allowed myself to forgive my mother's husband for what he had done because he had never accepted responsibility for his actions nor had he ever asked for my forgiveness. And honestly, I had never reconciled my mother's reaction to the truth and down deep I was harboring resentment toward her as well.

Attendance at my grandmother's funeral presented a very real challenge to me. As soon as I realized the predicament that I had placed myself in, my ever loyal sister-in-law, who lives in San Antonio, offered to house me and protect me. But I declined. I knew that I needed to face them, all of them—even if it meant facing all of them at the same time.

My sister Sofie and I quickly started making arrangements for my grandmother's service. Because she had been bedridden in her final years, my grandmother didn't belong to a church. Fortunately, my mother had been attending services at a very small church in Pearsall, Texas. She asked us to contact the pastor of the church to determine what scriptures would be read and what songs would be sung at the service. Sofie and I went and met the pastor. I should tell you that at first I was taken aback because the church building was a very small, Little-House-on-the-Prairie looking church, and when we arrived the pastor was outside in jeans and a T-shirt feeding a couple of stray cats. He had longish hair and tattoos. He walked toward us with a limp and extended a hand in greeting.

I can't tell you how comfortable he made us feel. He shared that his church was a very small church with just a few members. He said that his members were mainly those that others had thrown away and no longer wanted or needed. He said that his members were usually the drug addicts, the alcoholics and the forgotten. When I asked him if they had any space that we could host a little meal in after the service, he quickly offered a detached building located behind the church. As he let us in, he explained that the building didn't have air conditioning and that the building was actually used to provide Sunday school to the children on Sundays and Wednesdays. As I looked around, I saw evidence that, indeed, children were being taught the Good Word there. The walls contained taped pictures of Bible characters that some young children had colored. One of the rooms contained several little desks and a bookshelf with storybooks, a few Bibles and art supplies such as crayons, markers, and pencils. There was a little CD player with some Christian music CDs lying beside it. The main room was narrow and contained two old couches and two long tables. There was a kitchenette with a stove, a fridge, and a sink. All in all, it was very minimal, old, and outdated, yet abundantly sufficient.

Sofie and I agreed that with a little elbow grease and Pine-sol we could make it work. As we were leaving I asked the pastor if he wouldn't mind saying a prayer before we left to gather supplies and he graciously agreed. He prayed for my grandmother, my mother, my sister Ani, my brother Junior, my Uncle Alfred, and then he added a petition for healing and protection for all of us. With that, Sofie, my brother-in-law, Raul, and I headed to find someone to cater the meal. If you have ever been to Pearsall, TX you would know what a difficult chore that is. Our choices seemed to boil down to chicken or chicken. So we went with chicken. Not knowing anyone in Pearsall, I called my friend Lorena, who lives in San Antonio and who had never even met my grandmother, to ask if she wouldn't mind preparing some rice and beans to go with the chicken. Without hesitation, she agreed. My cousin Belinda and her husband brought bread and jalapeños and Ani and Junior brought some *pan dulce* from the local bakery.

The reason I am going into such detail is because I need you to know that His hand was definitely involved from the beginning. All of this happened in less than 24 hours. When my Cuban friend Rachel called to check up on me, I recall telling her how very sobering and humbling the whole event was for me. Because she is familiar with my past, she laughed and said, "Good. I was just checking in on you in case you had to go Cuban on them."

When I returned to my mother's house, I noticed everyone was unusually quiet. No one wanted to have to tell me that her husband was going to be attending the funeral. I walked into my mother's bedroom and I saw how worn out she was. On that day, I could really see how the years had taken their toll. Her room was dark and she had the air conditioning window unit going because it was over 105 degrees outside. She got up out of her bed and said that she needed to talk to me. She stood right beside me and held my hands and said, "Mija, I know that you don't understand why I still talk to him and I don't expect you to. You think that I don't love you and that I have chosen him over you, but I haven't. What you don't understand is that he is also Junior and Tilla's father. If I reject their father and join you in your hatred and anger for him, I am telling them that a part of them is hateful and worthless. And it's not that I think they are more important than you are but they need me more than you do. You have always been able to handle things in your own way. You have always known who God is, and you have Mike. They have nobody. And maybe I'm wrong, I don't know. But please, please don't leave here angry. Tomorrow I am burying my mother and I want you to be there but I understand if you choose not to." With that, she laid back down to rest.

I walked out of her room and headed back to San Antonio where I was to meet up with my baby sister, Tilla. Tilla is my youngest sibling and I absolutely cherish her. She and I have a very special relationship. She was born when I was eleven years old. In those days, my mother was so ill that she was unable to adequately care for Tilla. So when Tilla came from the hospital, I woke with her in the middle of the night to feed her, I changed her diapers, and I watched her grow into the beautiful young woman she is today. Tilla is fiercely protective of me and I of her. En route to San Antonio, I thought about what my mother had said and I decided to ask Tilla. I asked her, "Tilla? How does it make you feel that I never see or speak to your father? I mean, does it really matter that I refuse to be in the same room with him or that I have never allowed any of you to speak his name in my presence?"

Her faced turned pale and eyes started to water immediately. "Oh, Lisa," she started, "you know I would never turn my back on you and that I would never choose anyone over you. But I do sometimes wonder: when you look at me, do you see a part of him? The part of him that you hate and that you can't forgive? I wonder if you ever think that I am bad because I am his."

I felt as if I had been punched in the stomach. I placed my hand on my chest and the tears rushed through me like a tsunami. I pulled her to me and hugged her as tight as I could, and I said, "No! If anything you are the best thing he ever did. You and Junior are mine. I love you both so much. You can never, ever think that again!" And as we held on to each other and cried, I knew that the tide had changed.

On the morning of the funeral, my nephew Cruz and I walked into the church just as the service was about to begin. And as I was about to sit, Sofie leaned over and whispered, "By the way, you have to get up and say something about Grandma in a minute." What? Whatever happened to giving a person notice so that I could adequately prepare?

My Uncle Rey called me to the front within the next few minutes. As I walked to the front, I could feel my hands trembling. There I was in a church in the middle of Pearsall, Texas, with my grandmother in her casket in front of me. All four of my siblings, Sofie, Ani, Junior and Tilla and several of my nieces and nephews were sitting on the left side of the church. Sitting in the first two rows on the right side of the church were my unbelievably resilient mother, my surviving tias and great tias, my Uncle Rey and Aunt Sara, and my Uncle Alfred. And right there with them in the middle of the family section was my mother's husband.

I opened my mouth to try to speak, but the words were trapped in my heart. My Uncle Rey, who was standing beside me, put his arm around me and said, "Praise Jesus." Praise Jesus? Praise Jesus. Yes, that's right. That's what I decided to do. I decided to praise Jesus. I gently told my Uncle Rey that he had better take a seat because we were going to have church in there. And we did. I felt His words come up through my chest and I experienced a tremendous wave of relief as I stood up there and proclaimed in a strong voice, "My God is good!" My God is the God of grace and mercy and kindness. I claimed his victory over my life and challenged everyone else to do the same. I don't know how, but 1 John 1:9 just rolled off my tongue, *"If we confess our sins, He is faithful and just and will forgive us our sins and purify us from all unrighteousness."* I felt an urgency to share all of this because the death of my grandmother signified the end of an era for my family and me. I had come full circle, just as I had started my career as a migrant worker alongside my precious grandparents, there I was, standing beside my grandmother's casket still working as a migrant worker—just in a very different capacity.

I could tell that everyone was listening because everyone straightened up and I could hear the "Amen"s coming my way. I went on and discussed all the lessons that my grandparents' hard life and strong work ethic had taught me. I urged the young people to stay in school and learn new things but to never forget the lessons we had received about our family history, culture, and heritage. I asked them to remember the things we had been taught such as being respectful of our elders, of watching after each other, and of having good manners. I assured them that even from the hardest beginnings, life could still be beautiful. I acknowledged that being poor is difficult and often results in the occurrence of so many bad things that it sometimes makes it easier to make bad choices and huge mistakes.

I challenged everyone there not to forget where we come from and to not live in shame but to seek and give forgiveness and to live well. I reminded everyone that God can and will forgive, but that forgiveness doesn't mean that the consequences of sin simply vanish. Forgiveness doesn't justify behaviors or undo the past, but it does provide an opportunity for healing and permission to start enjoying your present and your future.

Before that moment, when I thought of my mother's husband, only bad, negative images would come to mind. But on that day when I looked at him, I saw an old man. A weak, hurt, tired, and physically handicapped man. I saw a man living in poverty with no one to really care for him and I felt-- *compassion*. Compassion because I know that revenge is not mine. One day he will have to make things right with God. But on that day, I witnessed his suffering and did something to relieve it. I forgave him. He didn't ask for forgiveness, but I forgave him anyway. I could tell by the look on his face that he knew our battle was over.

I don't plan to speak to him or to ever allow my children near him. Every choice has a consequence and he is still responsible for the consequences of his choices, but I too have a choice, and I choose to be free.

Sleeping with the Angels

Right now as I write this, I am in my car with my son and daughter as my nephew, Cruz, drives us to the airport to pick up my husband, Mike. He is returning from a medical mission trip to Mindo, Ecuador. I am anxious to hear of his adventures there. I am excited to learn of the ways he witnessed God's goodness through his interactions with the people of Ecuador. You may have been wondering why I rarely mentioned him throughout this book. The truth is that very little in my life happens without Mike in it because he is that big a part of who I am today.

At the beginning of this book, I mentioned a story about crying myself to sleep at night because I didn't know where the angels slept. That feeling of fear and of being lost and alone dominated much of my young life. Nightmares ruled supreme over every moment of sleep I tried to steal. Every noise would cause me to jolt up in panic. I spent much of my life in a state of anxiety. I trusted no one and had an ever present sense of foreboding. I immersed myself into my work, my studies, and my Kappa Delta Chi. Periodically I would allow myself to date someone. Unfortunately, those relationships were doomed from the beginning. I could only allow myself to stay in the relationship for so long. I could not and would not allow myself to open my heart and feel. And I certainly never shared my past with anyone. Up until that point in my life, I had told no one of my horrible, shameful past. I had comforted myself with the knowledge that God was the only thing I needed in my life.

And God in all His goodness sent Mike back into my life. Mike and I met when we were children. Mike grew up with his grandparents in Tahoka, Texas. My grandparents knew his grandparents and we would stop by their house when we were in search of migratory work in the area. Mike is a little younger than I am but we did have an opportunity to be in the same homemaking class when we were in junior high school. Very coincidentally, our homemaking teacher married us as part of an assignment in that class. How was I to know that he was going to take our vows so seriously!

Even though I was not allowed to go anywhere, Mike and I were "going out" intermittently throughout junior high and high school—that is, whenever we still lived in his area. He had an uncanny ability to just show up wherever I was whether it was at the grocery store or driving right behind me as I went to Dayton's Pharmacy on my bike. The interesting thing about Mike is that he doesn't just talk, he mainly listens.

Mike unfortunately became witness to some of the abuses present in my home life simply by being around when my mother would have her meltdowns. And even though I am certain that he must have thought our lives strange, he never said a word, and he never got scared. He simply remained loyal. It is no wonder that he was the first person I ever trusted enough to reveal my secret to.

A couple of years after I had joined the military and was well entrenched in university life, Mike reentered the scene. He had come looking for me one Spring Break while I was out of town and had asked my roommate to give me the message— the rest is the proverbial history.

On March 14, 1992, I married Mike and, in essence, his family. His family embraced me and loved me. His grandmother, Grandma-Grandma, treated me as her own. She was the kindest woman I have ever known. She once told me that she loved me as her daughter and I know with all my heart that it was the truth. My mother-in-law and father-in-law, even though they were divorced, approached all family affairs together. They couldn't get along for two minutes but they could never stay apart. Even though they weren't really sure what to make of me, they accepted me. Mike's siblings, Missy, Cynthia, and Edward, have always treated me with a tremendous amount of respect and love and I am blessed to have them as part of my family.

Life as my husband has not been easy for Mike. I have a strong will and attempts to tame me are met with forceful resistance. If I decide to do something, then it is done. I am often my own worst enemy and I find it necessary to constantly be thanking God for saving me from making irreparable mistakes. As I have sought significance in my life, he has patiently sat back and allowed me to search. He loves me and trusts me to make choices that will benefit our little, precious family. I am human and prone to making mistakes, just as everyone is, but he always picks me back up and allows me to get myself back together as he quietly goes about his business. His belief in me has strengthened my desire to honor him, love him, and be there for him when he needs me. I will always be grateful that he was able to recognize gifts in me when no else could, to see beauty in me when I felt worthless, and that he was willing to carry both of us when my wings were broken.

I don't exactly know when it happened, but I do know it happened. My husband in his own special, introverted, never pushy, sarcastic and often-questioning-God way guided me to a place of safety. Thanks to him, I now know where the angels sleep. I know the place where sweet dreams prevail and the angels watch me in my slumber. Our life together hasn't been a walk in the park, but when I watch him being the awesome father that he is to our two children, I am comforted in knowing that I am where I am supposed to be. I don't know how God plans to use me as I go forward, but in the meantime I plan to keep the faith, work hard, serve others, and live a life...*dulcified*!

About the Author

Dr. Lisa R. Ramírez is currently assigned to the United States Department of Education in the Office of Elementary and Secondary Education as the national director of the Office of Migrant Education in Washington, D.C. Dr. Ramírez is also a private speaker, consultant, and educator. Her primary focus in her private business is to promote educational leadership and the building of strong individuals and families through the convergence of different avenues that include family values and beliefs, cultural competency, education, resiliency, spirituality and service to others. She has had the privilege and the pleasure of seeing how education can truly help break the cycle of poverty by serving as a student, classroom teacher, assistant principal and principal in West Texas. Her experiences include working with high-risk populations that include minority,

EL, economically disadvantaged, special education and migrant students. Dr. Ramírez received her doctorate in Educational Leadership from Texas Tech University and her certifications include English, Spanish, English as a Second Language, Mid-Management and Superintendent. She is also an alumnus of the John F. Kennedy School of Government at Harvard University.

Her presentations have been made nationwide to a variety of audiences that include: universities, school board associations, teacher organizations, school districts, school campuses, youth groups, parent groups, leadership summits, service organizations, cultural competency work groups, church and community organizations, at-risk retreats and research associations.

To inquire about scheduling Dr. Lisa Ramírez to speak or to request additional information, contact her at:

Email: olive13paloma@yahoo.com
Twitter: @lisarramirez
Blogsite: www.olive13paloma.blogspot.com
Website: www.olive13paloma.com

47096303R00095

Made in the USA
Charleston, SC
29 September 2015